Date Due

101
MOST
POWERFUL
PRAYERS
IN THE
BIBLE

This Large Print Book carries the
Seal of Approval of N.A.V.H.

101
MOST
POWERFUL
PRAYERS
IN THE
BIBLE

Steve and Lois Rabey
General Editors
and
Claire Cloninger

Thorndike Press • Waterville, Maine

Published in 2005 by arrangement with Warner Books, Inc.

Thorndike Press® Large Print Inspirational.

The tree indicium is a trademark of Thorndike Press.

The text of this Large Print edition is unabridged.
Other aspects of the book may vary from the original edition.

Set in 16 pt. Plantin by Carleen Stearns.

Printed in the United States on permanent paper.

Library of Congress Cataloging-in-Publication Data

Cloninger, Claire.
    101 most powerful prayers in the Bible / Steve and Lois
Rabey, general editors ; and Claire Cloninger.
      p. cm.
    Includes bibliographical references.
    ISBN 0-7862-7225-2 (lg. print : hc : alk. paper)
    1. Bible — Prayers. 2. Bible — Meditations. 3. Large
type books. I. Title: One hundred one most powerful
prayers in the Bible. II. Title: One hundred and one most
powerful prayers in the Bible. III. Rabey, Steve.
IV. Rabey, Lois Mowday. V. Title.
BS680.P64C58 2005
  242′.722—dc22   2004061514

This book is lovingly dedicated
to my parents,
Charles and Virginia de Gravelles

As the Founder/CEO of NAVH, the only national health agency solely devoted to those who, although not totally blind, have an eye disease which could lead to serious visual impairment, I am pleased to recognize Thorndike Press★ as one of the leading publishers in the large print field.

Founded in 1954 in San Francisco to prepare large print textbooks for partially seeing children, NAVH became the pioneer and standard setting agency in the preparation of large type.

Today, those publishers who meet our standards carry the prestigious "Seal of Approval" indicating high quality large print. We are delighted that Thorndike Press is one of the publishers whose titles meet these standards. We are also pleased to recognize the significant contribution Thorndike Press is making in this important and growing field.

Lorraine H. Marchi, L.H.D.
Founder/CEO
NAVH

★ Thorndike Press encompasses the following imprints: Thorndike, Wheeler, Walker and Large Pr int Press.

Acknowledgments

You will meet many of my friends and family members on the pages of this book. That's because I almost always learn the greatest lessons on my spiritual journey from those I know best. And so I give special thanks to my husband Spike, my son Curt, his wife Julie, and their children Caroline and Jordan; to my son Andy, his wife Jenni, and their children Kaylee and Drew.

Special thanks go to those from whom I have learned about prayer, especially the Christ Anglican Church prayer team: Conlee and Signa; John and Laura; Tim; Betsy; Emilie; and Pam. And thanks to those who have allowed me to share what I have learned — the women's groups who have opened their hearts to me.

Thanks to my agent, Greg Johnson, at Alive Communications for his encouragement, to Steve and Lois Rabey, and to the good people at Warner Faith books, especially Leslie Peterson.

Contents

General Editors' Preface

There are thousands of verses in the Bible. How can we find the ones containing the divine wisdom and guidance we are looking for in order to help us grow spiritually and live more faithfully? This book and others in The 101 Most Powerful series will help you find and unlock powerful passages of Scripture that inspire, comfort and challenge.

The *101 Most Powerful Prayers in the Bible* helps us open our hearts to God by showing us how earlier saints and sinners prayed.

The 101 Most Powerful Promises in the Bible brings together those passages that convey God's boundless and eternal love for his creation and his creatures.

The 101 Most Powerful Proverbs in the Bible will enable us to apply God's timeless truths to many of the messy details of daily life.

And *The 101 Most Powerful Verses in the Bible* provides a treasury of divine insight gathered from nearly every book of the Old and New Testaments.

If author Claire Cloninger's name sounds familiar, you've probably heard some of the many award-winning songs she has written or read some of her previous books.

Claire brings a zest for life and a zeal for God to the readings that follow. On one page she draws fresh meaning from Bible passages that many of us have heard millions of times before. On another, she reveals some of the life-changing spiritual lessons that arise from some of the seemingly mundane events of daily life.

This and the other books in this series will never replace the Bible, but we do hope they will help you grasp its powerful and life-changing lessons and better utilize its wisdom in your life.

Steve and Lois Rabey

Introduction

In his book on prayer, Richard J. Foster referred to the heart of God as "an open wound of love." He described the Father as the one who "aches over our distance and preoccupation" . . . who "mourns that we do not draw near to him" . . . who "grieves that we have forgotten him."[1]

Seeing the heart of God from this viewpoint is compelling. How could we not rush headlong into the arms of the God who loves us so much, the one who longs to commune with us? How can we realize that he is waiting daily to meet with us, to speak to us, to hear us? And yet in our busyness we rush right past him.

God will not force us to return to him from our worries and concerns, but he will continue to draw us to himself. Even now he is inviting us to learn the language of the Spirit, to come to him through the doorway of prayer.

There are many facets to the language of prayer. To pray is to open our lives to

God's overcoming love, which is continually reaching out to us. It is to communicate from the heart with him as our most trusted Friend. It is to worship him for who he is, to sing with joy to him, to thank him for his blessings, and to cry out to him in our pain and grief. It is to confess our sins and receive his forgiveness, his restoration, and his healing. It is to seek his guidance and wisdom when we feel lost or confused. And it is to embrace the practice of intercession as we go to him on behalf of others.

But prayer is not merely telling God how things are with us and asking him for what we want. It is also learning to listen to God in the quiet places of our hearts as he reveals how things are with him and tells us what he expects from us.

The Bible is the ultimate textbook on prayer. There are literally hundreds of examples of people who have met their challenges by praying. And there are the prayers themselves — the book you are holding contains 101 such prayers. Many are presented with examples of how these prayers have affected my life or the lives of loved ones and friends. I pray that everything the Lord has led me to include in this book will enrich your own prayer life as it draws you closer to God.

Before I close, I feel compelled to add that we will never learn all we need to know about prayer by reading about it. We will learn best to pray by praying.

Father, bless us as we begin. We long to know you in a deeper way. Teach us to love you through the language of prayer. In Jesus' name, amen.

1

Return to the Garden

A broken and contrite heart,
O God, you will not despise.

Psalm 51:17

Once there was a garden where prayer flowed like rivers, where thanksgiving sprang up like grass, and worship fell like morning rain. In that garden, that distant land, that long-ago paradise, a friendship with the Father was the most natural thing on earth. In that garden we walked and talked with God.

That relationship was the one for which the Creator designed us. And although it contained everything we would ever require for fulfillment and joy, we let it go. We let it slip away. We let go of love and touched temptation and the garden vanished.

Now many times we move through our lives without even realizing that the most essential part of who we are is missing, like a phantom limb. We experience an aching emptiness at the center of ourselves we can't quite express. As we navigate snarled

21

lanes of traffic, juggle the minutiae of our jobs, work at being the best parents, children, or friends we can be, we know that something fundamental is missing. As we try to pull together the hundred loose ends of our lives that should provide meaning, we so often come up empty.

Even we Christians, who know on some level that we are God's forgiven children, find ourselves longing for a deeper sense of connectedness with him; a deeper sense of union.

How can we reclaim the sweet intimacy of the Garden of Eden — the place where the man and the woman walked with God in the cool of the day without shame and with total abandon? How can we move into that place again?

God is showing us the way. He has left us every clue to his presence and every evidence of his yearning for us, like scattered bread along the path of prayer. He is waiting for us to come with broken spirits and contrite hearts. He is drawing us to himself, saying, "Here I am. Come to me.

"Come with a trusting heart like David when he prayed, 'Because you are my help, / I sing in the shadow of your wings' [Ps. 63:7].

"Come with a surrendered heart like

Mary when she said, 'May it be to me as you have said' [Luke 1:38].

"Come with a thankful heart like Paul when he praised me as the one who is able to do 'immeasurably more' than all he could ask or imagine [Eph. 3:20].

"Come home, my child. I am waiting."

O Lord, thank you for inviting us to pray. Thank you for calling us back to you: out of our weariness into your rest, out of our need into your abundance, out of our loneliness into your friendship. Continue to draw us to you. Teach us to pray. Amen.

2

A Primer on Prayer

This, then, is how you should pray:
Our Father in heaven,
hallowed be your name.

Matthew 6:9

Prayer is the gateway to God's heart. Who better to open the gate for us than the Son whom he loved? Who better to give us instruction on prayer than the one who lived by prayer, the one who did only what he saw his Father doing — the one who said only what he heard his Father saying?

The first line in the Lord's "primer on prayer" settles several of our most basic issues of faith. Whose father are we talking to? Is he someone else's father or ours? Is he someone we know only from a distance? Is he a father we can trust and call on in a time of trouble, or is he some capricious deity who is playing tricks on us? In this first line we learn that he is our good Father.

I know my human father well. He loves me and takes pride in me. Whenever I was in a play or a recital, he was there. Mom said he enjoyed sitting somewhere near the front, and at some point during the performance he would inevitably point me out to another parent sitting nearby. "She's ours," he would say, "third from the left."

Dad also found ways to include me in his grown-up world. I remember him letting me sit in his lap and steer our old maroon Ford coupe when I was only four or five. Of course we only went up and down the driveway, but in some way I felt he was handing over a special adult responsibility to me, and I loved it.

If God is *our* Father, he's like that. He is up close and personal. He's in heaven, yes. But he did not stay at a distance. He came to earth to walk the human journey alongside us through the life of his Son.

"Hallowed be your name." In the time and the culture of our Lord, to speak someone's name was to speak of his character. To some extent this is still true in our time and culture. If you say that someone smeared your name, you are saying that the other person had smudged your reputation or character.

Hallowed is another word for *holy,* so to say "Hallowed be your name" would be the same as saying "Holy is your name" or

"Your name is holy."

Putting these definitions and "translations" together enables us to come up with one of the most basic phrases of worship in the language of prayer. "Hallowed be your name" could be translated: "Lord, our God. Your character is holy. Your personality is pure and precious and without flaw. Holy is your name, O Lord. Holy is your name."

The next time you say the Lord's prayer, don't let that first line slip by without realizing what you are saying:

Our Father, the God who loves us, the one whom we can trust and turn to — our Father, your home is in heaven but it is also in our hearts. Your name and your character are holy and righteous and without flaw. Amen.

3

Wanting His Will

Your kingdom come,
your will be done on earth as it is in heaven.
                                    Matthew 6:10

There is a perfect plan in the Father's heart that he designed for you. One of the surest ways to keep moving toward the Father and his plan is to agree with his will for you.

Many characters in the Bible wanted only their own wills and their own ways. Far fewer desired the Father's plan, but they were the spiritually powerful ones. Here are a few of them and their prayers:

Mary, after hearing the angel's prophecy regarding the child that she would bear, prayed, "Let it be to me according to your word."

Though David had sinned and moved away from God's plan for his life, he finally came to a place where he repented (turned around) and this was his prayer: "Teach me to do your will, for you are my God; may your good Spirit lead me on level ground" (Ps. 143:10).

Jesus himself, who desired his Father's perfect will more than anyone, prayed near the end of his life that the bitter cup of God's will would be taken away. But later that same evening, when he prayed for a second time, these were his words: "My Father, if it is not possible for this cup to be taken away unless I drink it, may your will be done" (Matt. 26:42).

God has a design for us each day. We can miss it or we can find it. If we miss it, it is our loss, not his. If we find it, it is our gain.

If you have not the vaguest clue as to what God's will is for you, you may not have been listening carefully enough. God wants to communicate with us. He wants desperately for each of us to hear him.

And what he has for each of us will not be drudgery. It will not be boring. We won't feel like we are scrubbing floors while everybody else is going to the ball. It will be exactly right for us.

But we will never find his will for us until we are willing to "seek and knock and ask." Until we are willing to say as David did, "Teach me to do your will," we'll remain on the outside looking in.

Father God, I want your will because I know that nothing else on earth will truly fulfill me.

28

Forgive me for trying to satisfy myself with the bland food of my self-will when you are waiting with the banquet of your perfect will for me. Amen.

4

The Prayer of "the True Bread"

Give us today our daily bread.

Matthew 6:11

My daughter-in-law Julie made fresh home-made bread every day for the first five years of her marriage. Having been the recipient of many of those fragrant, nourishing loaves, I know what a gift they were — especially in this era of mass-produced food.

When Jesus told us to pray to our heavenly Father daily for the nourishment that we require, he was communicating on more than one level. He was telling us to seek God for physical food — the vitamins, minerals, grains, and vegetables — our bodies need. But he was concerned with much more than that.

More than what we find in the amply supplied bakery departments of our local supermarkets, more than the homemade tortillas that are mixed and patted flat with the dirty hands of women along city streets in Third World countries, more than the unleavened bread of sacred ceremonies,

God wants to supply us with the bread of his presence, the nourishment of his friendship. He wants to meet us in our times of prayer and enter into a personal relationship with us.

For he has said that "man does not live on bread alone, but on every word that comes from the mouth of God" (Matt. 4:4). Jesus knew what it would take for us to survive in life. We were created for a relationship with him and with his Father.

To feast on the true bread of the Lord's friendship is to experience spiritual satisfaction, to know an inner sufficiency as God supplies all our needs. It is to find every yearning filled with his nearness, every question answered by his love.

Jesus was the Word incarnate who was with God from the beginning. "Through him all things were made; without him nothing was made. . . . In him was life, and that life was the light of men" (John 1:3–4). Who is more qualified to know the requirements for our survival?

On a mountainside by the Sea of Galilee Jesus demonstrated his power to supply a symbol of what he would later call "the true bread" (John 6:32). There, surrounded by a hungry crowd, he took five small barley loaves and two small fish and fed an enormous crowd. Five thousand people ate and twelve baskets were filled with leftover pieces.

That night Jesus went out to a boat, but the people refused to let him alone. They tracked him by land first, and then by sea. When they finally found him in Capernaum, they asked, "Rabbi, when did you get here?"

Jesus answered, "You are looking for me, not because you saw miraculous signs but because you ate the loaves and had your fill. Do not work for food that spoils, but for food that endures to eternal life, which the Son of Man will give you" (John 6:25–27).

In prayer we feed on the Bread that is essential, the True Bread that endures through to eternal life.

Father, I thank you that you desire to feed me with the "true bread" of your Son, for he is the "food" that endures. I receive the bread of his presence into myself — body, soul, and spirit — with joy and gratitude. Amen.

5

Choosing to Forgive

And forgive us our debts, as we also have forgiven our debtors.

Matthew 6:12 (NIV)

At a women's conference recently I had an opportunity to pray with a woman I'll call Marcia. She was beautiful, well dressed, and confident-looking. Only the pinched expression around her mouth betrayed any hint of her real outlook on life — Marcia was choked with resentment.

Angrily she spewed out the story. After twenty-seven years of marriage, her husband, Lee, had fallen in love with a woman half his age. With hardly a second thought or a backward glance, Lee had left not only Marcia and their three children but their hometown, his insurance business, and a pile of unpaid bills.

"At first I was consumed with grief," she said. "I cried nonstop. Now I'm so angry I feel that if only I knew where he was, I would do something very violent."

I couldn't lecture this hurting lady. I

33

didn't have her problems. But I did tell her a powerful story I once heard at a conference led by Christian speaker and conference leader Clay McLean, a story that helped me understand one reason the Lord so strongly urges us to forgive.

Once after Clay spoke on forgiveness, a very angry woman approached and told him at length why she had no desire to forgive the people who had made her life a living hell. It seemed her two older stepbrothers had sexually abused her every night from the time she was eight until she was sixteen and she finally left home. Clay stood there horrified by the wrong done to this sad woman. "Lord, what can I say to her?" he silently prayed. And then it came to him.

"And they will continue to abuse you every night until you choose to forgive them," he said firmly. "Forgiving them is not to imply that what they did was okay. It means only that you're releasing them and their sin to God's judgment so you can get your life back."

As I told this story, the light dawned on Marcia's face. She could see that she had imprisoned herself by her unwillingness to forgive Lee. She was ready to forgive.

We knelt together and thanked the Lord

for the gift of forgiveness. Then I prayed for Marcia to have the strength to forgive her ex-husband.

"Lord," she prayed with tears in her eyes, "I choose to do it your way today. I choose to forgive Lee. And if my anger returns tomorrow, help me do it all over again. But for today, I choose to forgive."

Lord Jesus, thank you for your sacrifice on Calvary, making a way for us to be forgiven and teaching us how to forgive. We choose forgiveness because it is what you have prescribed for us. Work through us, empowering us to be instruments of your forgiveness. Amen.

6

The Bad News and the Good News

And lead us not into temptation,
but deliver us from the evil one.

Matthew 6:13

In his book *Telling the Truth*, Frederick
Buechner related an incident in which the
well-known preacher Henry Ward Beecher
traveled to Yale University to deliver the first
of the Beecher Lectures, a series established
in honor of his late father.

Beecher passed a troubling night because he had no idea what he would say.
The next morning as he shaved, suddenly
it came to him.

Staring into his own eyes, he knew that
his life had become a farce. He thought of
the furor that was brewing in his own
parish, the results of his own actions:
gossip, tales of adultery, tearful confes-
sions. And he was at the center of it all. At
that moment, Beecher's razor slipped, and
he cut his face. He wrote notes for the
sermon in his own blood!

What a dramatic picture of coming face-to-face with our own sin. As Buechner put it, "Well the old pulpiteer might have cut himself" because his lecture came from "the deep trouble that he was in or the deep trouble that was in him."[1]

There is deep trouble in us all — trouble that we may manage to turn our eyes from . . . until that day when we are shaving or putting on lipstick and suddenly there it is — staring us in the face.

Read the Bible and you'll meet the cast of characters on every page: This great march of humanity. This great parade of sinners. From Adam to Paul, with the exception of Jesus himself, all of them weak and faulty and fallen and frail. All of them in need of a Savior.

And unfortunately, sin is an ongoing predicament. Our susceptibility to it never goes away. That's why Jesus taught his followers to pray, "Lead us not into temptation and keep us from the evil one."

But there is an awesome postscript that comes on the heels of the bad news. It is the good news of Calvary.

Buechner put it this way:

The Gospel is bad news before it is good news. It is the news that man is a sinner . . . that when he looks in the mirror all in a lather what he sees is at least eight parts chicken, phony, slob. That is the tragedy. But it is also the news that he is loved anyway, cherished, forgiven, bleeding to be sure, but also bled for.[2]

Oh, Lord, how good you are to us, your children. We let you down and still you love us. We fall and you lift us up. Forgive our sins today, Father, and deliver us from the evil one. Amen.

7

I Will See Your Face

Show the wonder of your great love. . . .
And I . . . will see your face.

Psalm 17:7, 15

Have you ever longed to see Jesus? Really see him? These words from my husband's journal describe the day Jesus "showed up" at a high school track meet when Spike was least expecting him.

Saturday, May 3: "The stadium was filled with track teams from all over the state . . . the bright colors of their running clothes like a patchwork quilt spread out in the sun."

Then Spike described a two-mile race in which a large number of runners — the best two from each district in Alabama — competed. He explained that usually there were not large gaps between the finishers, since all were state-qualifying runners.

But for the Alabama School for the Deaf, this was not the case. Their two runners finished dead last, almost a full lap behind the winners. I watched these two strong, handsome teenagers cross the track after the race, eyes downcast in embarrassment. Climbing the steps, they were the essence of broken spirits.

Suddenly, bounding down the steps to meet them came their coach, a plump little man, a good two inches shorter than either boy. As the two runners approached him on the stairs, the first one raised his head and looked at the coach with such an expression of brokenness on his sweating face that I could scarcely bear it, and the second young man actually backed down a couple of steps.

Reaching the first runner, the coach enfolded the boy with an enormous hug. Then looking him directly in the face, he spoke these words very distinctly and loudly: "You did a fine job in running that hard race. I love you and I'm very proud of you!"

The runner looked unblinkingly at his coach's mouth, straining to read the words on his lips. As their meaning gradually dawned, I watched a smile cover his face — a smile that was a joy to see.

The coach then bounded down the steps to where the second runner waited to face criticism. The coach spoke loudly enough for anyone within fifteen feet to hear: "Martin, I'm proud of the race you ran. I told you we could have our best time and we did. I love you and I'm proud to be your coach."

As he turned and accompanied the boys up the steps, patting them all the way, I could see that they were totally transformed, their exhausted bodies straight, their heads held high with renewed strength and confidence.

And so once again I saw him. Jesus. Clothed in green and yellow polyester shorts, with a stopwatch around his neck, coaching deaf runners in Troy, Alabama, in broad daylight for anyone to see.

"I love you and I'm proud to be your coach" is what he said.

Oh, Father, this world so desperately needs to see your Son. Let it be through us. Amen.

8

A Prayer for Unity

May the God who gives endurance and encouragement give you a spirit of unity among yourselves as you follow Christ Jesus, so that with one heart and mouth you may glorify the God and Father of our Lord Jesus Christ.

Romans 15:5–6

Our two sons, Curt and Andy, twenty-one months apart in age, were not born with a natural affinity for each other. I guess you could say they were wired differently. They had different kinds of friends and listened to different kinds of music, and by the time they had reached high school, the differences had begun to create a serious rift in what had always been a pretty rocky relationship.

I tried to encourage them to be kind to each other, but you can imagine how much difference a mother's interference made: little to none. So they basically agreed to disagree and our family bumped along like a car with sand in its gas tank. And it broke my heart.

The longer we lived like that, the more I understood how the Father must feel as he looks down on his world and sees our inability to mend our fences and love one another. I suddenly noticed how many brother relationships were in the Bible — from Cain and Abel, who got it all wrong, to Peter and Andrew, who got it all right. And I intensified my prayers for Curt and Andy, that they would eventually learn to love one another.

God did not answer those prayers in a day or an hour. But I can tell you about the breakthrough moment when I first felt hope. I was in the back of our house in my bedroom, alone for all I knew. Suddenly I heard men's voices coming from the den. I remember thinking that Spike must have brought home some of the men with whom he was working. I walked to the den to say hello and there sat my sons conversing with one another in the most civilized way.

I backed out as quietly as I could, hoping that they had not seen me or the stunned look on my face. Returning to my room, I sat on my bed in a state of mild shock and wept with joy. I really did.

Years have passed since that pivotal moment. My sons are still unique people. But they love each other now. They are friends.

And they have a Friend in common who has made all the difference.

Father, thank you for giving us the endurance and encouragement we need to love one another as brothers and sisters in the truest sense. Knit our hearts together in the bonds of your Son, Jesus. Give us one mind to know him, one heart to love him, and one Spirit to praise him forever and ever. Amen.

9

A Little Chip of Grace

The grace of the Lord Jesus Christ be with your spirit. Amen.

Philippians 4:23

Most of us can remember moments of grace that came to us through people in our lives before we had ever heard the Word. One such example I can remember occurred when I was only six years old.

My first-grade classroom was filled with marvels: a fish tank, an easel with paints, but best of all, my teacher's rock collection. Some afternoons Miss Sullivan allowed those of us who had finished our work to go quietly to the back of the room and look at the rocks. My favorite rock was a crystal pink one that sparkled in the afternoon light.

One day, quite inexplicably, I reached out, picked that rock up, and put it in my pocket. Sick with guilt, I rushed home and threw myself into my mother's arms. "Oh, Mama," I blurted out, in tears, "I took Miss Sullivan's rock and you're going to have to take it back."

Mama could have lectured and scolded but she could see that I didn't need to be convinced of my guilt. So instead, she held me until my sobbing had subsided. Then she drove me back to school to face the consequences of my behavior.

There are times when "dying a million deaths" doesn't nearly describe it! I felt so wretched I could hardly breathe. My teacher was still at her desk, grading papers. When she saw me, she held out her hand. The distance between the door of my classroom and my teacher's desk seemed like a million miles. With my head hung down, I walked it.

"I'm the one who took your rock, and I'm so sorry," I confessed. I silently waited for the reprimand I knew I deserved. But it never came. Her grace met my confession and I found myself bathed in forgiveness.

Instead of scolding me she did something I will never forget. She opened her arms to me and enfolded me in them. Then she took my hand and told my mom that we would be right back. Hand in hand we walked to the school's little supply room where we found the janitor, Mr. Pete.

"Pete," she said, "I want Claire to have a

little piece of this rock to keep. Do you think you could chip one off for her?"

"I think I can do that," he said. And that's exactly what he did.

Over the years that crystal pink rock has been like a little chip of God's grace. Like my Savior's love, it is a gift I didn't deserve from a friend of whom I was not worthy.

Perhaps there is an incident of grace in your own life that still glows like a candle on a dark night. Thank the Lord for it and never let it go out. Instead spread that flame from heart to heart until many walk in the light of his gracious love.

Oh, Father, make my life a testimony of the grace you show me in daily ways. Thank you for the ultimate gift of grace that continually flows into my life through the shed blood of your Son. I pray this prayer in his name, amen.

10

A Powerful Pattern for Prayer

Answer me when I call to you,
O my righteous God.
. . . Be merciful to me and hear my prayer.
Psalm 4:1

Although we know that every Christian's
"job" is to pray, many of us would rather do
something more dramatic or important. To
us prayer sometimes seems very small on the
scale of Christian accomplishments. But
Jesus does not see it that way. To him prayer
is everything: "a duty as well as a privilege, a
right as well as a responsibility."[1]

How many times I have heard people
say, "The least we can do is pray." Just the
opposite is true. The most we can do is
pray. So why is it that many of us have de-
veloped such anemic prayer lives? Perhaps
it is because no one has taken the time to
teach us.

I have found Pastor Bill Hybels's simple
formula for prayer a helpful one. He based
it on the acronym ACTS. Each letter rep-
resents a recommended ingredient of our

daily prayer time.

A stands for *adoration.* In his book *Too Busy Not to Pray*, Hybels stated that beginning with adoration is essential because it sets the tone for everything that is to come. Adoration is a time to worship God for his attributes, his holiness, his character, and his personality.

C stands for *confession.* Hybels suggested that confession is one of the most neglected areas in personal prayer. All too often we clump our sins into one big stack of dirty laundry and label them "all my many sins." What a cop-out! We must get particular with God about each sin, not only asking him to forgive us but also asking him for the strength to turn away from them.

T stands for *thanksgiving.* Hybels recommended thanking God specifically for answered prayer, spiritual blessings, relational blessings, and material blessings.

And finally *S* stands for *supplications* or requests. "If you have adored him, confessed your sin, and thanked him for all his good gifts, you're ready to tell him what you need," wrote Hybels.[2] God cares about our every need and desire, large and small, and he wants to answer our requests.

Hybels concluded this teaching by recommending that we write out our prayers using the ACTS pattern. By dividing a piece of paper into four sections and labeling each section with one of the letters, we can see the particulars of our adoration, confession, thanksgiving, and supplication as we lay them before our Father in prayer.

Father, we thank you for the gift of prayer. Teach us how to go deeper and reach higher as we come to you each day. In Jesus' name, amen.

11

A Prayer for Honest Work

*May the favor of the Lord our God rest
upon us;
establish the work of our hands for us —
yes, establish the work of our hands.*

Psalm 90:17

My son Curt made an interesting comment recently. "I'm afraid that we are becoming a race of 'virtual' men and women," he said, "doing no real physical labor, only sitting in front of our computer screens, tapping keys, sending our putty-soft bodies out on virtual expeditions."

I knew what he meant and that it was true. Last night after working into the late hours on this book, I lay in bed and could not rest. Something was wrong. What was it? Flicking rhythmically behind my closed eyelids was a cursor. I could not turn off my internal screen!

This morning when we were sitting on the porch at our river house, Spike read to me from Wendell Berry's book of short stories, *Fidelity*. In "A Jonquil for Mary

Penn" were beautiful descriptions of work — real physical work. I love this one about Elton Penn's plans:

This morning, delaying his own plowing, he was going to help Walter Cotman plow his corn ground. [Mary] could feel the knowledge of what he had to do tightening in him like a spring. She thought of him and Walter plowing, starting in the early light, and the two teams leaning into the collars all day, while the men walked in the opening furrows, and the steady wind shivered the dry grass, shook the dead weeds, and rattled the treetops in the woods.[1]

And I loved this section about women on a day of berry picking: "And there on the ridgetop in the low sunlight they danced the dance of women laughing, bending and straightening, raising and lowering their hands, swaying and stepping with their heads back."[2]

As I listened to Wendell Berry's simple, musical descriptions I was moved by the beauty of the words. I almost felt a desire to pull on a pair of overalls and head out to walk the opening furrows of the fields with Elton and Walter. Or to grab my berry basket and go out picking berries with Josie Braymer and Mary Penn and the others.

Wendell Berry's descriptions reminded me, too, of the year we built our cabin here in the woods: of the morning we stood on the new foundation with Spike's parents and prayed for a sturdy structure, a place where the whole family could share laughter and togetherness. His descriptions reminded me of the hard physical labor that left us happy and exhausted, and of the day that the work was finally completed.

But this is another day and I have another kind of work to do. Still, I can do it with the same simplicity and diligence and I can find joy in it, because the Lord is in it with me. So with the blinking of a cursor in my eyes and thanksgiving in my heart, I offer this work to him.

Father, thank you for the work you have given me to do. Use it to bless your people and bring you glory. May it be a testimony to your grace in my life. In Jesus' name, amen.

12

A Prayer of Weeping

Hear my prayer, O LORD,
listen to my cry for help;
be not deaf to my weeping.

Psalm 39:12

In every life there will be times of weeping —
crushing disappointments, heartwrenching
realities that wrap us in betrayal and rob us
of our joy. There will be times when the
bridge ahead of us caves in and we can't go
forward, and other times when the road behind us disappears and we can't go back.

It could be a broken relationship that
leaves us feeling as frail as a butterfly's
wings. A move to a new city might make us
feel like aliens on a yet undiscovered
planet. It could be the death of a loved
one, an illness, an addiction, or the loss of
a job.

I am thankful for the prayers of David.
They let me know I'm not the only one
who's ever had a broken heart — not the
only one who has lain across the bed
weeping — not the only one who has felt

alone and brought my brokenness to God.

I don't pretend to know what makes you cry. I seem to cry more when I'm misunderstood than when I'm physically wounded. I cry for starving children with their shriveled limbs and pleading eyes looking out of the television screen and for those who are dying today in countries where the gospel isn't preached. (And then sometimes, before my tears are even dry, I turn off the television set and forget to write the check.)

I have cried at the deathbed of my sister and at the marriages of my sons — for the beauty and the brevity of life.

And I cry when I feel alone. I hug my solitude to myself like a badge of uniqueness. "No one has ever felt so lonely," I say wordlessly.

I have felt alone in huge crowds of people at concerts or sporting events, looking around at them and wondering, *Am I the only one who feels this way?* I have felt alone at times in foreign countries where the customs and the culture aren't mine. And I've even felt alone in my own hometown in my own home church with my own best friends. I have felt alone when I have needed God and was too brokenhearted to put words to my prayer.

Whatever the cause, he has always dried my tears . . . always drawn me close. And his promise to me is that in the end he will dry every tear from every eye (see Rev. 21:4). That's why I know without a doubt that I can trust him. I can let my tears flow in his presence and be certain he will take care of them.

O Lord, thank you for giving me permission to feel my feelings. Thank you for welcoming my emotions. Thank you for the shoulder of a father on which I can cry. And though I sometimes feel alone, thank you for the awesome reality of your ever-present love. In Jesus' name, amen.

13

A Woman of Beauty

I will be glad and rejoice in you;
I will sing praise to your name,
  O Most High.

Psalm 9:2

I wish you could see my friend Jessie praise the Lord. I wish you could watch the glow on her face as she tilts her head back as though she is gazing into heaven itself. If her unself-conscious praise blesses me this much, how it must bless the Lord!

How can I describe Jessie as unself-conscious? How do I know that she is not conscious of herself? Because Jessie is blind. She cannot see you seeing her. And besides that, she doesn't care. Long ago Jessie chose to cast her gaze on the Lord rather than worry about the opinions of other people.

What kind of life does Jessie lead? She is a widow. She lives alone. She has learned to count the number of steps from room to room and to gauge the distances between the contents of her house. But Jessie does not merely subsist in a limited existence. She is rich in all of the important ways.

She's a woman of prayer with a heart full of joy. She sings in the choir and laughs with her friends. She has a faith that reaches out to others. She teaches the Bible to two younger women in her neighborhood who come to her home one day a week.

I was privileged to be part of that study one day, and I saw firsthand the way these younger women look up to Jessie — the fondness and admiration in their eyes. (Once again, she was unaware of herself. She was there to usher them into the presence of her Lord. And she did.)

When I see Jessie's face, when I encounter her faith, when I join her in prayer, I feel ashamed that I spend any time at all thinking about outward appearances. The loveliness I see in Jessie's life is the kind that Peter spoke about when he said, "Your beauty should not come from outward adornment, such as braided hair and the wearing of gold jewelry and fine clothes. Instead, it should be that of your inner self, the unfading beauty of a gentle and quiet spirit, which is of great worth in God's sight" (1 Pet. 3:3–4).

Jessie is that kind of woman. Her prayer, her praise, her life itself are beautiful in

God's sight. And in mine.

Oh, Father, thank you for the strong women of faith and beauty you are raising up in the body of Christ. Thank you for their courage, their faith, and their gifts. Thank you for the example they hold up to those of us who are blessed to know them. Help me to walk in the joy and integrity that they model for me. Amen.

14

All the Wonders of Your World

How many are your works, O Lord!
In wisdom you made them all;
the earth is full of your creatures.

Psalm 104:24

I have just come in from a walk by the bay.
The wind was whipping up the waves, the
clouds were gathering in great dark clusters,
and all the seabirds — pelicans and gulls and
two great blue herons — seemed to know a
storm was coming.

I never tire of watching a pelican set his
majestic wings like sails, rising, soaring,
and dipping high overhead like a kite on a
string. I believe that in a way God was
showing off on my walk. I could feel him
there, taking pride in his creation as he
showed me the approaching storm.

"Oh, Father!" I wordlessly prayed. "What
an awesome God you are!"

Since the days of Eden, God has found
joy in sharing his world with his children.
The more we appreciate the wonders of his
world, the better we know him. The better

we know him, the more we love him. And the more we love him, the more we find our lives on the course for which he designed them.

What does he want to share with us? Open your eyes and ears and heart. The evidence of his love in the creation is all around. Don't miss a single opportunity for praising him as your Creator, or thanking him for what he's done.

It's "little" things like the look of wonder on a baby's face as she takes her first wobbly steps toward her parents, and the sound of her chuckle as she realizes that she has actually done what she set out to do. She may see only her earthly mother and father. But her heavenly Father is there too, cheering her on. Can you see him there? He wants you to.

It's the colors in a garden — the oranges and blues and cream-colored blooms pushing their way into the world for the first time like the fulfillment of a promise. But he treasures more than the garden itself. He treasures the gardener, too, the one who dreamed up its beauty and set the seeds in the ground and watered and waited for the blooms. Can you see the garden and appreciate the gardener? God wants you to.

And he wants to share with you his greatest possible joy, a friendship with you. He wants to talk with you, to listen to you, to hear your prayers, to dry your tears, and to mend your heart. Can you allow yourself to believe that? He wants you to.

Oh, Father, I worship you! Thank you for opening my eyes to your miracles, large and small. Thank you for walking beside me, sharing the beauty of your world. Thank you for the gift of prayer and the friendship you are holding out to me today. Amen.

15

A Stream of Prayer

Hear my prayer, O LORD;
let my cry for help come to you.
Do not hide your face from me
when I am in distress.
Turn your ear to me;
when I call, answer me quickly.

Psalm 102:1–2

When I was a child my family stayed at a wonderful summerhouse in northern Louisiana called The Wind Blows Inn. An ankle-deep stream ran in front of the tree-shaded cabin, and some of my most delightful childhood memories are of playing with my siblings and my cousins in that stream. It eventually joined Cassan's Branch, the big swimming hole, but by using branches and rocks we could dam up the natural flow of water and create our own little floating pools.

Sometimes I look at my prayer as a stream of conversation like that stream in which we played. Some days it flows effortlessly. The words and yearnings of my spirit move so naturally to the great ocean of God's mercy that I feel us becoming one.

On other days it's as though something has dammed the flow of my prayer and formed stagnant pools inside of me. Selfishness or envy or some other sin has caused my prayer to double back on itself rather than flow on toward its heavenly destination.

At times like that I'm convinced that God's face must surely be turned away from me and my prayers have become like David's in Psalm 102. They have echoed down the well of my despair: "Is anybody there? Does anybody hear me? SOS, God! Answer me!"

Whenever we feel that God has turned away from us, it's good to know that he hasn't. Whenever we are reaching out to God we will find him reaching out to us. He's always waiting to hear our prayers — to bring about the restoration we long for, the reconciliation we require.

Jeremiah 33:3 reminds us that when we call to God he will answer us. He will tell us "great and unsearchable things" that we do not know. I want to know those deep things that God has reserved for me. I want to hear those beautiful secrets that he is waiting to whisper in my spirit. Don't you?

God has a covenant to keep with each of us. If you are reading these words I know that God is not through with you. He has not turned his back on you. How do I know that? If you are still alive, he is still working in your life. Let him kick down that dam and get the streams of prayer flowing in your heart again!

Dear Father, thank you that we don't have to drown in our sinfulness. Thank you for your Word that promises a life of new beginnings in Christ. Keep the streams of my prayer ever flowing toward the ocean of your mercy and the grasp of my faith ever reaching toward the hand of your grace. Amen.

16

All Called to Be Pauls

O LORD, let your ear be attentive to the prayer of this your servant and to the prayer of your servants who delight in revering your name.

Nehemiah 1:11

What is the cry of every Christian mother's heart? That her child may come to know Jesus as Lord. What is the prayer of the Christian son or daughter at the bedside of a dying parent? That this one who brought them into the world may not take the final breath before he or she knows Jesus. What is the desire of one who knows life's deepest answer for the friend who is still seeking? That the seeking friend may come to a knowledge of Christ.

Isn't this the core of all intercessory prayer? As we bend our knees and lift our hearts in prayer to our Father, the essence of what we are seeking on behalf of those for whom we intercede is that they would know him, believe him, and trust him completely with their lives.

Who are God's intercessors? He can use anyone and wants to use everyone. Paul, for instance, was a very unlikely candidate. He was one of the most ardent persecutors of Christ's fellowship, and yet he became an intercessor and an evangelist extraordinaire (see Gal. 1:13–24).

Our music minister was feeling a special need for prayer. Our youth group took the initiative of sitting at the front of the church for several months to intercede for the worship team, the choir, and the music minister. What a powerful difference they made! Our musicians felt a new freedom to worship and minister. And the worship itself seemed to soar.

Each of us has a territory, an area of influence in which God calls us to be an intercessor (a "Paul," so to speak). We may be called to intercede for children in our neighborhood. We may coach a neighborhood baseball team. We may run errands for an elderly neighbor and keep her in our prayers as we do.

One year our friend Gail White, a teacher, had a particularly difficult sixth-grade class. She gave each of us in our prayer group five names, urging us to intercede for those children each day. She was amazed at how quickly the spirit of her classroom began to turn around as we daily brought her students before the Father.

My daughter-in-law Jenni gave me a ribbon-trimmed bulletin board for Christmas this year. I knew immediately what I would use it for. I hung it near the spot where I pray and attached recent photos of all the missionaries we support. Now I'm reminded daily to intercede for them. Foreign missionaries desperately need our prayer, not only for their ministries but for their physical safety and that of their families.

When I go out to speak to women's conferences, I rely strongly on the intercessory prayers of others. My vision, my wisdom, my message, my strength are only as powerful as the women who stand behind me in prayer. I would not dream of trying to face down the darkness unless I knew that committed intercessors were at home lifting me into the Lord's light. These women are the "Pauls" in my ministry. Lisa, Pris, Susan, Renee, Jacque, Nancy — I couldn't do it without you!

Father, I pray that you would first open my own eyes to the needs around me: those of family, friends, acquaintances, our nation, and the world. Then give me the heart of an intercessor so that my prayer, empowered by your Spirit, may bring many into a knowledge of your perfect Son. Amen.

17

A Silent Song of Praise

Be exalted, O God, above the heavens;
let your glory be over all the earth.

Psalm 57:11

That first day after hiking eight miles from the rim of the Grand Canyon to the Colorado River below, my eyes had seen more beauty than I could have expected. My body was trembling from the punishment it had taken. Some kind person helped me put up my tent and I fell into a deep, dreamless sleep like a rag doll falling into a black hole.

Then at some point during the night I awoke to what seemed to be a gigantic flashlight in my eyes. My heart was pounding and I was unable to remember where I was. The source of light? The full moon had arisen over the rim of the canyon and was perched just above the unzipped flap of my tent.

Then I remembered and leaned back on my pillow, feeling the strangeness of this new place. I let the impressionistic memory of the day flow over me like colors on a canvas. The shades and the shapes. The sounds and the silences. How incredible that I was actually there!

I had intended to journal every day, but I had not. I determined then to take better notes the next day. But as the days progressed I couldn't find the words. Or perhaps I didn't want to. The words seemed to make less of the experience rather than more. They seemed to strip it of its majesty. I was almost afraid that my impressions would escape if I tried to trap them in the verbal prisons with which I was so familiar. Even my prayers had become a silent song of praise. And finally, I surrendered to the canyon itself and let it do its unspoken work.

Since that trip I have never forgotten the sense of silent awe I experienced there. It was like a face-to-face meeting with the one who spoke to Job from the whirlwind — the God who said,

"Where were you when I laid the earth's foundation? . . . On what were its footings set, / or who laid its cornerstone — / as the morning stars sang together / and all the angels shouted for joy?" (Job 38:4, 6–7).

71

No wonder Job stood speechless.

Like Job I had no words. . . . only the shifting colors of the sunlit canyon walls. Only the roaring of the river as we ran the rapids. Only my own quiet breath of praise.

Father, thank you for the song of the canyon, for the majestic praise of your creation that is all around us. May we hold in our hearts your perspective — that you are the one who made everything from nothing, blessed it all and called it "good," and we are your children. Amen.

18

Behind Closed Doors

On my bed I remember you;
I think of you through the watches
of the night.

Psalm 63:6

Several years ago I was asked to be part of a seminar on healing prayer at Trinity Seminary in Ambridge, Pennsylvania. Ambridge, once a bustling steel town, is now a shell of its former self with many closed buildings.

One day as our group was driving through the town, I noticed a church building that was shut down. On the front door hung a huge "For Sale" sign.

I remember thinking what a sad metaphor that was for what is taking place on many levels in the church today. Many of us have shut down the spiritual rooms of our lives. We are even selling them out to the highest bidder in a world of superficial, economic idols.

Why has our culture become such an unfriendly habitat for the spiritual man or woman? Why do we find ourselves caught in a noisy, busy existence, always reaching and striving, but finding it difficult to experience the quiet oneness with God for which we were created? It makes you wonder: Is there still a quiet place where we can meet with him?

Many Old Testament writings placed God in a physical setting. The Book of Isaiah, for instance, speaks of the Almighty enthroned between the cherubim in the temple (Isa. 37:16). The Books of Leviticus and Numbers lay out very precise and complex rules for approaching God in his sanctuary. In the Psalms we discover that David was one Old Testament believer who had a very personal prayer life. He spoke of crying out to God all night long on his bed (Ps. 6:6).

And now because of what Jesus did on the cross, the veil of the temple has been torn, releasing New Testament believers from the limits of praying to God in specific physical settings. We can communicate with him anywhere!

In fact, Jesus recommended that we go into our own room and close the door to pray. "Then the Father, who sees what is done in secret, will reward you" (Matt. 6:6).

There is no showmanship in a prayer behind closed doors — no playing to the crowds as the Pharisees often did. Behind closed doors prayer becomes a totally private affair.

When we are willing to reserve the quiet center of ourselves for the awesome presence of God, we will know the intimacy and power of a private prayer life.

Dear Father, we know that we were born not for the doldrums of this world's daily-ness but for the richness of your Spirit adventure. Forgive us for selling out. Give us the courage to tear down the "For Sale" signs on our hearts and freely open them to you. Teach us to go into our private rooms, to close the door, and to pray. Please, Lord, meet us there. In Jesus' name, amen.

19

A Prayer for Our Children

We constantly pray for you, that our God may count you worthy of his calling, and that by his power he may fulfill . . . every act prompted by your faith. We pray this so that the name of our Lord Jesus may be glorified in you, and you in him.

2 Thessalonians 1:11–12

I remember so well the weekend we drove our son Curt to Sewanee, Tennessee, to begin his freshman year at the University of the South. We deposited a jumble of clothes, track shoes, and books in his first dorm room and said our good-byes, which seemed all too brief.

Though I knew Curt was where he had worked very hard to be and I was proud of him, I also felt like my heart was breaking. All the way home in the car I played Wayne Watson's song "Watercolor Ponies," about how the sweet moments of child-hood must come to an end. I was grieving the end of an era.

The morning after that long, sad trip I

called my mom, who is often my best ther-
apist. She could tell I was at rock bottom.
"What is it?" she asked.

"Oh, Mom," I sobbed, "it's over."

"What's over?" she asked.

"You know," I said, "the whole parenting
thing."

"Trust me," she said with amusement in
her voice. "It's never over!"

How true I have found that to be!
Though both our sons are grown now,
both married to wonderful women and
doing a great job of raising their own children, we are still their parents. We try not
to butt into their affairs with unsolicited
advice, but when they come to us for help,
we are here for them.

But beyond any hands-on help or verbal
advice, there is one way we stay involved in
their lives, their decisions, their marriages,
their child rearing, their jobs — and that is
through prayer. Each morning we lift them
in prayer to the Father who loves them
more than we do.

And what do we seek for them in prayer?
We seek the same blessings that Paul
sought for the Thessalonians: that they will
remain true to their high calling in Christ
as they are constantly emptied of their own
willfulness and filled with his Spirit. We

pray that God will fulfill every good purpose for which he created them, and that
his amazing love might make them alive —
this love that is greater and more gracious
than we can comprehend.

*Father, bless our children. Bring forth the highest
and the best in them. Reveal to us our roles in
their lives as the kind of parents you would have
us be. Help us not to worry or to meddle but to
pray. We trust you with their lives. Amen.*

20

A Thirst for God

O God, you are my God,
earnestly I seek you;
my soul thirsts for you, my body longs for
* you,*
in a dry and weary land
where there is no water.

Psalm 63:1

I remember my first experience with a desert. Our family traveled from the lush, green vegetation of the Louisiana Gulf Coast where I was raised to the empty, sometimes monochromatic horizon of the American West — a setting of sand the cactus plant only occasionally broke up. As a child who was accustomed to green trees, colorful flowers, and flowing rivers, I felt the desert was very unwelcoming.

Sooner or later, every human heart will experience its desert seasons. Even the most sincere believer will know times when the lushness and beauty of a rich prayer life grow stale and colorless. Rivers dry up. Flowers fade. And the green leaves that had given us shade fall to the ground, leaving our souls exposed to new and brutal rays of reality.

How do we approach God in these desert times? There may be a temptation born of pride to hide our thirst — to bring God only our abilities, our solutions, our strengths, our works. We may find ourselves wanting to disguise our neediness under the camouflage of our "Sunday best" by polishing our spiritual shoes and coming into his presence as though we, in our humanity, actually had something to offer him who is divine.

The truth is, all we ever have to bring to him is our emptiness, our lack, our nothingness apart from his all. All we ever have to bring is our total need for him in our lives.

David never resisted that deep and troubling truth. He understood that there was a hole in his heart that only God could fill. And he rushed toward the Source of his healing. Because David had many sins, he never lost touch with his thirst for God's mercy.

If you're not in the desert today, simply thank the Lord for his goodness to you and then intercede for someone who is. But if you are in that arid landscape, don't try to camouflage your need. Learn the lesson of the thirsty heart. Cry out to the Lord as David did and know that your prayer will be heard.

Father God, I thank you for the seasons of my journey — for the times of sorrow and the days of joy. Thank you that you are with me through it all, drawing me ever more deeply into your reality, meeting my needs, and using every conflict to teach me new things. Father, increase my thirst for you. May I never be content with where I am, but may I ever desire to know you more. In Jesus' name, amen.

21

Becoming His Glory

My plea is not for the world but for those you have given me . . . they are my glory.
John 17:9–10 (author's paraphrase)

The words of John 17 provide an opportunity to eavesdrop on a song that Jesus was singing to his Father — a love song of unity.

"You and I are one, Father," he sang. "All I possess is what you possess. The ones I love are the ones you love — these men and women and children who love you and honor you and live their lives for you. These are my glory."

My brother-in-law Curt is a Christian writer and actor. Curt and his friend Geoff Koehler wrote a dramatic piece entitled *When I Died Last Tuesday* about *being* God's glory. In it a famed theologian has died and is seated in heaven's outer office. There he is informed that he will be reading the best of his twenty-two scholarly works to Jesus and a roomful of the world's most acclaimed theologians.

The titles of his books roll over in his

mind. Which one will Jesus select?

Finally he is ushered into what looks like a playroom. There, seated on the floor, is a very familiar group: Martin Luther, Mother Teresa, Dietrich Bonhoffer. Jesus beckons the theologian to join them. Nervously, he does.

A small, folded piece of paper is passed to the theologian from the back of the room.

"What is this?" he asks Jesus.

"Your greatest work," the Savior responds. The theologian unfolds the paper and finds inside a poem he once wrote and hid in his daughter's lunch box when she was eight years old.

He is furious. He feels as though the Savior is teasing him. But as he reads aloud the childlike poem he recognizes the delight in the eyes of his listeners. They applaud as Jesus reads the last verse along with him.

"I don't understand," the theologian says. "All the years of study and tedium. Twenty-two books. Was it all for nothing?"

"Did you enjoy it?" Jesus asks.

"I loved every minute of it," the theologian answers.

Jesus pauses. "Did you ever love it more than you loved me?"

Tears fill the theologian's eyes as he understands his Savior's question.

I've probably seen that piece performed half a dozen times, and it always hits me with a fresh poignancy as I learn again the lesson of the theologian. Jesus has called me "his glory." I must let go of trying to love him with my accomplishments rather than letting him love me with his grace. I must let go of trying to produce some works for his glory rather than simply *becoming* his glory through my faith.

Father, I thank you for the prayers of your Son. Thank you that he sees each of us as his glory. Thank you for the unity we enjoy with him when we realize that we are in him and he is in you. Amen.

22

A Threefold Benediction

May the grace of the Lord Jesus Christ, and the love of God, and the fellowship of the Holy Spirit be with you all.

2 Corinthians 13:14

As we share our daily lives with one another, there is no more powerful prayer we can extend to one another than this spiritual blessing. Though it is brief, it is a benediction that offers so much of what each of us needs in order to live in peace and harmony as God's children.

The first part of the threefold benediction is grace. The grace of the Lord Jesus demonstrates his generous nature and his capacity to forgive in this sinful world that so desperately needs to know him. It is the infinite love, mercy, favor, and goodwill poured out on humankind expressed in God's sending his only Son to die for undeserving men and women. When we speak this benediction of the Lord's grace upon fellow believers, we are reminding them that God gave the powerful gift of his

Son while they were yet sinners. When we speak it to those who do not yet know the Lord it becomes an invitation to know him.

The second part of the threefold benediction is love — the love of God. To look at the life of Jesus is to gaze into God's love. His love was patient and kind, not envious nor boastful nor proud. It was not rude, not easily angered. It was not self-seeking and it kept no record of wrongs. His love did not delight in evil but rejoiced in all truth. It always protected and trusted and hoped and persevered. All we have to do is look at the Cross to know that this love never failed and it never will. The love of God is the greatest of all virtues (1 Cor. 13:4–8, 13).

The third part of the threefold benediction is the fellowship of the Holy Spirit. This is the completing virtue that flows through us when we accept Jesus Christ as Savior and Lord. He prays and loves through us via his Spirit. The Spirit is rooted in the eternal nature of God — he is one with the Father and with the Son, and as a result of our faith he becomes one with each of us. He is the Counselor whom the Father gave to remind us of everything in his name (John 14:26).

As we send this threefold benediction around the world to God's children everywhere, we are extending the essential, sacrificial, and gracious nature of our God. There is no greater blessing.

Father God, we do ask that the grace of your Son, Jesus, along with your own powerful love and the fellowship of your Holy Spirit, be with each member of the body of Christ today. And may this powerful benediction create in many unbelievers a hunger to know you. Amen.

23

The Prayer of a Trusting Spirit

But I trust in you, O LORD;
I say, "You are my God."

Psalm 31:14

There is nothing quite so peaceful as a sleeping infant, hands uncurled, the quiet sound of his deep and even breathing. I recall so many afternoons standing beside the cribs of my babies and glorying in the benign state of their comfort as they napped.

In those early months of their lives I took delight in the fact that I was doing my job well. I was what I had always longed to be: a good mother.

As my children grew, I had to do what every mother must: begin to let them go. In elementary school we allowed them free rein in the municipal park directly behind our house. But they were never to venture out as far as the street that led to the lake.

During the middle school years their freedom grew by increments. Little by little their boundaries expanded and my nerves became more rattled. I began to fear that they were slipping from my grasp, so I tried to tighten it. When Spike was working out of town (which he was, more and more) I became the little lady they could take advantage of. I made demands; they made jokes. I pushed my agenda; they pushed my buttons. It was not an enjoyable time in my life to say the least.

By the time they were full-fledged teens I was more or less a nervous wreck. All this time I was a Christian, but during these years my prayers were far from faith-filled. I had begun to fret and pout.

"God," I would pray as I paced and worried, "you have *got to* help me. You have *got to* help this child. You have *got to* do this and you have *got to* do that." ("In the name of Jesus," I would add testily.)

I was nagging God with full-fledged fear and panic. I couldn't rest until everyone was in the house at night, so I was getting very little sleep.

It was not until I began attending a twelve-step program that I learned there is a name for people with behavior like mine: *codependent.* A codependent person is one who desperately tries to control everything and everyone in her life. As she becomes obsessed with clutching the problems of others, she loses her ability to help herself.

During that time I was also introduced to a wonderful slogan: "Let go and let God." In short, this means *trust God*. As I gradually began to open my hands and release my loved ones into the strong, loving care of my heavenly Father, he was able to take his rightful place in all of our lives and bring his solutions into our family.

Dear Father, I thank you that I can trust you and rest in you. I place my needs and concerns and my loved ones in your hands. And for this one day, I choose to leave them there. Amen.

24

Choosing the Best

And this is my prayer: that your love may abound more and more in knowledge and depth of insight, so that you may be able to discern what is best and may be pure and blameless until the day of Christ.

Philippians 1:9–10

Why do we pray for God's gifts of insight and knowledge and wisdom in our lives and in the lives of those for whom we intercede? Why do we want his love to abound in all of us? Is it merely for our own personal enjoyment? No, there is a higher motive. We want to be able to discern God's design when we face decisions and choices.

I understood what Pastor Phil Ware meant when he stated:

I don't know about you, but my most difficult decisions are not about choosing between good and bad. I usually know what is good and what is bad, especially when bad involves evil. My toughest choices are when I have to choose between good, better, and best.

My love for God usually overcomes my weakness and I choose good over bad. But unless I've placed myself before God's Word and surrendered my heart to him in prayer, I have a very tough time choosing between good and best.[1]

I have definitely found this to be true in my life. The enemy can rarely trip me up on the choices that lie between black and white. Where he gets me is on the choices that fall into the categories of gray. For instance, I would never get confused about the question of whether I should rob a bank or go to church. That's black and white. But gray areas might be whether to watch television or spend some time studying the Word; whether to go shopping or go to visit a friend in the hospital; whether to give the house a good cleaning or take a nap.

There is nothing wrong with watching TV or shopping or napping. The question is simply what would God have me do now? Or as the little bracelet puts it — WWJD? What would Jesus do?

I believe our Father wants to supply us with his love, his knowledge, and his insight so that we will be equipped to make the strongest possible choices in every area. How can we cooperate with God in his desire? Author Beth Moore suggested that we become strong "choosers" by "starving the flesh and feeding the spirit."[2] Feeding the Spirit involves plenty of time in the Word, in fellowship with other believers, and especially in prayer. As we follow this prescription we will find ourselves more and more able to choose not only what is good but what is God's best.

Father, I thank you for desiring wonderful things in my life. Enrich my study of your Word. Give me strong Christian relationships. And draw me into a deeper prayer life so that I may choose the best. Amen.

25

A Sister's Lessons

Teach us to number our days aright,
that we may gain a heart of wisdom.
Psalm 90:12

My sister Alix died on a Tuesday with clear, iridescent tubes in her arm dripping saline and morphine, neither of which yielded any help. Her skin looked porcelain and strangely angelic. Her bald head seemed as fragile and perfectly shaped as a bird's egg.

I remember thinking when she lost her hair what an injustice it was. On top of having to endure this killer disease, she also had to watch her lovely, pale hair fall out.

Her daughter, Jeanne, had helped her buy a wig before the first chemo treatment, but she hated those blonde curls. She nicknamed them "Harpo" and retired them to her closet, where they sat like a sad caricature of herself in happier days. Instead she chose to cover her head with a variety of hats and scarves that she wore with a great deal of panache.

I remember the day Mom first called to tell me about the diagnosis. She had trouble even saying the word *cancer*. It was almost impossible for any of us to connect that word to my sister, who was so full of life.

There were only five months from the day of Alix's diagnosis until the day of her death. During those months there was a trip to Houston for a second opinion and an appointment at the National Institute of Health in Washington, D.C., where Alix attempted to qualify for an experimental cancer treatment. Neither trip brought any new hope. And still she clung to life with every fiber of her being.

Alix spent as much time as she could with her children and grandchildren. Sometimes I would try to encourage her to rest, but it was as though her eyes were hungry for the sight of them. They energized her.

She was on a totally unappetizing macrobiotic diet someone had recommended. "Aren't you sick of this stuff?" I remember asking her.

She looked at me intently. "Claire, you still don't get it, do you?"

We stared at each other. "Get what?" I asked stupidly.

"How precious life is," she said, amazed that I could be so obtuse.

The truth is that no one truly "gets it" until it is ebbing away and we suddenly catch sight of its shimmering beauty. Most of us believe on some level that our lives will go on forever — until the diagnosis brings us face-to-face with our mortality.

That is why we need God's perspective so desperately! That is why our prayer must be "Lord, teach us to number our days aright that we may gain your heart of wisdom. Teach us to treasure our lives while we are living them."

Father, forgive me when I rush through my days, not appreciating, not seeing, not loving. Help me to walk with open eyes and an open heart. Give me your heart of wisdom. Amen.

26

Are You Listening?

Speak, LORD, for your servant is listening.
1 Samuel 3:9

In the third chapter of 1 Samuel we learn that "in those days the word of the LORD was rare; and there were not many visions" (v. 1). It kind of makes me wonder. Which came first — the fact that God wasn't saying a lot or the fact that people weren't listening? Which came first — the fact that people weren't looking for God or the fact that visions were rare?

God is a person like us, and I don't know about you, but when I know I'm not being listened to, I tend to clam up a little. When I know that no one cares whether I show up or not, I tend not to show up.

And yet the young boy Samuel heard the voice of the Lord when Eli, the temple priest, did not. Did you ever wonder why? The answer to that question, I believe, is that Eli was tuned out and Samuel was tuned in. Samuel was listening.

Samuel heard an audible voice and

jumped up to answer that voice. "Speak, Lord," he said, "for your servant is listening."

Is the Lord getting through to you these days? Is there an inner voice calling you? Do you know that voice? Do you recognize it? Are you responding with a ready answer, or are you rolling over in bed and going back to sleep?

It's so easy, so tempting, to ignore the voice that's calling. And yet it's important to realize that the more we do that, the more difficult it will become to hear that voice next time.

Because Samuel listened to the Lord, his power to hear and respond grew stronger. We are told in 1 Samuel 3:19 that "the LORD was with Samuel as he grew up, and he let none of his words fall to the ground." Samuel was not always popular with the people, but he always spoke what he heard the Lord saying in his spirit.

Are you listening for the voice of God in your spirit, the voice that brings God into every decision? As long as you are listening, he will speak. As long as your heart is tuned into his frequency, you can depend on him to touch you with his words of reason and his hand of wisdom.

In my prayer time, I often write in my

journal about a place of indecision. And after that I write, "Speak, Lord, for your servant is listening." Then after listening prayerfully, I often hear him do just that.

Oh, Lord, I thank you that you still desire to speak to us. Stir up in me a desire to listen. Quiet me in your presence. Quiet the voice of my own will so that I can hear your still, small voice. I love you, Lord. I long to hear from you. Amen.

27

An Intercessory Partnership

In all my prayers for all of you, I always pray with joy because of your partnership in the gospel from the first day until now, being confident of this, that he who began a good work in you will carry it on to completion until the day of Christ Jesus.

It is right for me to feel this way about all of you, since I have you in my heart.

Philippians 1:4–7

What higher calling is there than to pray for those with whom we colabor in the faith? God gives us the faith we require and the confidence we need to thank him for our "prayer partners" and lift up their needs. He gives us gratitude to thank him for the good work he has begun in them — a work he will carry on to completion until Jesus returns.

The secret of Paul's passionate intercessory prayer for his colaborers was his love for them. In his intercession he was shifting gears — changing his point of view from any and all needs of his own to the needs of others.

We must learn to make that shift in our own prayer lives as well if we are to become intercessors. There are so many desperate needs in the world today that require our prayer energy. Marriages are coming apart at the seams. Children are suffering from the breakup of the family system. Individuals are moving aimlessly from place to place like trains ripped free from their tracks.

As Richard Foster said in his book *Prayer: Finding the Heart's True Home,* "In the ongoing work of the kingdom of God, nothing is more important than intercessory Prayer. . . . We can make a difference if we will learn to pray on behalf of others."[1]

To be intercessors is to keep company with Jesus Christ. To follow in the Savior's footsteps is to live as he lived, and if we do, then we will know the joy of his reinforcing our intercessory prayers with his own. The writer to the Hebrews proclaimed that Jesus is an eternal priest who "always lives to intercede" for his followers (Heb. 7:25). And Paul assured us that Jesus Christ died, was raised, and is at the right hand of God, interceding for us (Rom. 8:34).

If you have not yet begun to keep a prayer notebook or journal, this is a good time to begin. Create tabs in your notebook for Worship, Confession, Thanksgiving, Answered Prayers, and Intercession. Ask the Holy Spirit to lead you and pray through you as you begin each day.

Oh, Father, teach us to be intercessors as Jesus was. Keep our hearts tender as we constantly lift your children in prayer before you. In Jesus' name, amen.

28

Beauty for Ashes

*[You] provide for those who grieve in Zion
. . . a crown of beauty instead of ashes,
the oil of gladness instead of mourning,
and a garment of praise instead of a spirit
of despair.*

Isaiah 61:3

My friend Candy was raised in the old section of Mobile, Alabama, with three sisters and a delightful mother named Janet Bartee. Janet's quaint, antique-furnished cottage was located directly across the street from the Old Springhill Cemetery, where the dates on some of the graves go back more than 150 years. When anyone died in Old Springhill you could count on loads of beautiful flowers being delivered to the gravesite.

As children Candy and her sisters looked at a funeral as an invitation to make bouquets for their mother. They would slip into the cemetery at night and select the blooms of their choices. Then they would take them home and create elegant floral arrangements. Janet wanted the girls to understand that the flowers were not their own personal property, but she just couldn't seem to fuss at her daughters about them. She couldn't help but admire their handiwork and so she gratefully received each floral tribute.

Besides, Candy's grandmother, "G'Ma," had always said, "Don't waste flowers on my gravesite when it's my turn to go — let someone else enjoy them. Flowers are for the living!" (G'Ma had owned a beautiful flower garden that she tended for the pure pleasure of it.)

So this past spring when Janet Bartee died, Candy and her sisters remembered their G'Ma's oft-repeated sentiment. They also remembered the pleasure Janet had taken in their bouquets, and they decided that everyone who attended Janet's funeral should take home the funeral flowers when the service was over in memory of their mother.

What a wonderful funeral that was! I was powerfully moved to hear Candy (who is now a missionary with her husband, Wylie, in Colombia) share memories of growing up in her mother's home. Then she closed by inviting all in attendance to come into a relationship with Jesus.

At the gravesite I realized that Candy

and her sisters were creating a beautiful tribute to their mom. What better way to honor her memory than to send each of us away with armloads of riotous blooms in every color of springtime? And I couldn't help but picture Janet's pleasure at seeing her girls bestow on each of us a crown of beauty instead of ashes, the oil of gladness instead of mourning, and a garment of praise instead of a spirit of despair.

My Father and my God, I worship you for the beauty of your world and for the personalities of those who take joy in it. I praise you for your gracious heart that wants to replace our grieving with delight. We give you all of our praise. Amen.

29

An Undivided Heart

Give me an undivided heart,
that I may fear your name.

Psalm 86:11

My poor parents lived through the mis-
adventure of raising a child who never knew
what she wanted. If any kind of choice was
before me, they knew they were in for
trouble. A cafeteria line was a disaster:
Green beans or mashed potatoes? Apple pie
or strawberry shortcake? And once I had
chosen, I often wanted to go back and make
an exchange.

Mama learned not to take me on shopping expeditions unless she was willing to
spend exorbitant amounts of time. Fortu-
nately I usually liked what she chose for
me.

One summer after I was in college, when
the family was taking a vacation, Mom and
Dad made the ominous error of letting me
choose whether to go with the family or to
stay in my hometown with a friend. I
changed my mind so many times that ev-

eryone was exhausted. In fact, Mom and Dad assure me to this day that they finally drove off with my packed suitcase in the car and me running behind, shouting, "Wait! Wait! I've changed my mind!"

God longs for us to be steady and secure in our thought lives, in our emotions, in our actions, and in our choices. This way of thinking and living comes easier and more naturally for some of us than for others. For this reason the Lord teaches us to seek him and petition him for "an undivided heart." This is a prayer that he desires to answer in every life, and his answer to this petition in every life can change it.

When David asked the Lord to grant him an undivided heart, he knew what benefit he was requesting. He was asking for the kind of heart and mind and personality that would reverence God's character and adhere to God's way of doing things.

An undivided heart is not a heart that turns this way and that, choosing one thing one minute and another thing the next. A person with an undivided heart has a heart like God's, a heart that is righteous and balanced and whole and holy. One of the most steady, balanced, and spiritually grounded people I ever knew was my mother-in-law, Marjorie Cloninger. I knew her all of my life and had been married to her son for well over twenty years at the time of her death, spending much of that time in her home. Never once in all that time did I see her faith waver or her sense of humor fail. Her secret? Marjie had an undivided heart that grew out of a life of prayer.

Because I long to live as Marjorie did, I often pray the words of Psalm 86:11. It is a prayer that I need to have answered every single day.

Oh, Father, you know how easily I am tipped off center. You know how easily I can become distracted and unfocused. I desire to be like you. And so I look to you again. Thank you for promising to mold me into your image as I seek you. I stand in awe of who you are. And I ask to be formed by your character. Give me an undivided heart. In Jesus' name, amen.

30

The Family Album

All the days ordained for me
were written in your book
before one of them came to be.

Psalm 139:16

What is my life — a brief span of days that only God can see? The days of my future are flung out before me like unread pages in a book; the days of my past, caught up in the wind of yesterday.

My prayers are in that book: those answered and unanswered, prayers of pain and prayers of rejoicing. With so many lives, so many pages, and so many prayers, how can God know them all? If all these details are really written in his great, infallible book as Psalm 139:16 suggests, it must be a very big one indeed, like a titanic textbook of facts and figures.

But every now and then something will happen to give me a glimpse into God's book as it really is. And I can see from his perspective that it's not an impersonal record. It is a family album. Let me share one such incident.

We were married six long years before we became parents, and during those childless years, I yearned for a baby so desperately I ached. One of my favorite songs during that time was sung by Barbra Streisand. It was called "Jenny Rebecca, Four Days Old." The lyric described a mother welcoming her little daughter to the world and it pictured all the wonderful things they'd be doing together: playing on swings and tree climbing and wishing on stars. How I longed for a little girl with whom I could share those kinds of things.

Of course my heart's desire changed the minute I held our first son. My dreams of pink frilly rooms vanished and my life was taken up with trucks and trains and bugs in a jar. Curt was the joy of our lives.

But after the wedding of our second son, Andy, God opened that big family album for me and allowed me to look over his shoulder at a tender and amazing answer to a long-ago prayer. As Jenni and Andy were signing their marriage license, I noticed for the first time that my daughter-in-law's full name was Jenni Rebecca, the title of the song I had sung so wistfully. Why hadn't I made that connection before?

"Jenni," I said, "I've never noticed your full name before. It's beautiful!"

"Oh," she said, laughing, "Mama named me after a song."

Tears sprang to my eyes. Here was the prayer our Father had always planned to answer. Here was the daughter our Father had planned to bring into our family to bless our son and nurture our grandchildren. She had been in the family album under the Cloninger name all along!

Lord God, thank you that you hold the details of our lives in your loving hands. You have gifts and treasures you will release to each of us in due season. Teach us to wait on you. Amen.

31

A Special Psalm

I lift up my eyes to the hills —
where does my help come from?
My help comes from the LORD,
the Maker of heaven and earth.

Psalm 121:1–2

Many years ago as a newlywed living in Fort Knox, Kentucky, I took part in an amateur production of *The Diary of Anne Frank.* Anne, you'll remember, grew up in a Jewish family in World War II Holland. Friends took in her family and hid them from the Nazis. The play followed the stresses and joys of the Frank family during their confinement, which Anne recorded in her journal, and it ended with their capture by German soldiers.

Though I would have preferred the role of Anne, I believe the Lord placed me in the role of Mrs. Frank for a reason. I was not a believer at the time. I did not know the Word of God. But my part required me to memorize the words of Psalm 121, which begins, "I lift up my eyes to the hills

— / where does my help come from? / My help comes from the LORD, / the Maker of heaven and earth."

By the power of the Holy Spirit, those words stayed in my heart between the time I learned them for that theater production to the time I came into a personal relationship with the Lord many years later. They became a prayer within me and a love song. In situations when I knew I needed help, those words flooded my mind and I would feel my spirit lifted in prayer to this God I had not yet come to know.

Years later, after surrendering my life to the Lord, I thought again of the words of Psalm 121 and I understood their meaning. That was when I realized that God had been answering that prayer in me according to his mercy for decades!

Following the World Trade Center attack of 2001, when Word Music commissioned me to work with Gary Rhodes in the creation of a new musical, we chose to base it on Psalm 121. Realizing how powerful and healing the message of this Psalm could be during the grief and challenge of America's difficult season, we wove familiar songs, hymns, scripture verses, and worship choruses together with our own original narrations and compositions. We invited listeners to lift their eyes to the God from whom our help comes, the God who is with us in every trial, the God who neither slumbers nor sleeps. As I sat in the sound booth listening to our musical, *Lift Up Your Eyes*, come to life, I praised God for bringing the prayer he had set in my heart full circle.

O Father, I lift my eyes to you. In you alone my help resides. I refuse to give up. I refuse to look at the darkness. Instead I turn constantly to the light that is in you and you alone. I lift up my eyes. Amen.

32

Don't Let the Stones Steal Your Song

*Blessed is the king who comes in the name
of the Lord!*

Luke 19:38

Will there ever be a situation in which the
Lord silences the praises of his people? Will
he ever say, "I've had enough! Quiet! Be still!
No more of your incessant worship!"

No! Never!

All we have to do is look at the events of
Palm Sunday recounted in Luke 19:37–40
to assure ourselves that Jesus will never
seek an end to our praise.

"When [Jesus] came near the place
where the road goes down the Mount of
Olives, the whole crowd of disciples began
joyfully to praise God in loud voices."
They sang, "Blessed is the king who comes
in the name of the LORD!"

But some of the Pharisees in the crowd
didn't like the noisy praises of the ram-
bunctious crowd. They said to Jesus,
"Teacher, rebuke your disciples!"

At that point Jesus spoke surprising

words to them. In effect, he replied, "If my disciples keep quiet, then the very stones on these hills will proclaim words of worship to me and to my Father. The birds in the air will join in accolades of alleluias to my Father's glory. This earth itself will rejoice in a song of glory, whether you decide to be part of their rejoicing or not. So do not try to still their worship."

He seemed to be admonishing them to make their own decision, saying, "Will you stand on the side of the worshipers or the side of the mockers?"

I believe that there are still those in the church who are trying to get the Lord to quiet the "wild worshipers," saying to him, "Teacher, rebuke your disciples!"

When praise takes on the passion of a parade, there are always people on the sidelines who say, "Lord, these disciples have got to get a grip! This is getting out of hand!" When the joy gets too joyful and the singing too ecstatic, there are always those who want to put the lid on.

But the Lord never intended to tame our hearts. He never meant for us to be repressed or docile or domesticated. Though there will indeed be times of quiet worship and reflection, he longs for a fervent display of our love for him. Worship is for the worshiper as well as for the Worshiped. Worship is a unique opportunity to connect with God intimately as his children, acknowledging him for his awesome qualities and his faithfulness. In worship we set things in perspective, saying, in effect, "you are God and we are not. We bow our hearts before you." As we give our hearts over fully to our Father in worship, we experience the purpose for which it was created.

Oh, Father, I desire to worship you with all my heart. Thank you that you have created me to worship. May my heart touch yours today as I lift my prayer of worship to you. Amen.

33

Following Directions

Show us your unfailing love, O LORD. . . .
I will listen to what God the LORD will say.
Psalm 85:7–8

When our son Curt was doing short-term mission work in the Caribbean, his team leader decided to have the team spend a day in worship and prayer, seeking God's will for their last port of call, St. Croix. It was during that special day of quiet that Curt distinctly "heard" the Lord tell him to make a banner.

The vision of that banner was beautiful, Curt said. It was gold and red and purple. There were small bells on it along with the words, "Jesus is Lord over St. Croix." On that same night, Curt got his marching orders for the banner: "Carry this banner counterclockwise around the outer edge of the island, and undo the curse over my people."

After that it was never a matter of figuring out what God wanted; it was just a matter of figuring out how to make it happen. That didn't take long. The next week, quite unsolicited, an anonymous check arrived from a church in Mobile for one hundred dollars and with it Curt bought the material. He had only $1.04 left over!

As Curt shared his vision of the banner with his team, everyone began to get excited. Everyone wanted to take part. A construction foreman on Curt's team came up with the idea of using PVC pipe for the frame and built it. One girl who had brought her sewing machine to the St. Croix base put the banner together. Another team member volunteered to paint the letters. Several different people volunteered to go on the walk.

There are many Scriptures about banners. Jeremiah 50:2 says, "Announce and proclaim among the nations, / lift up a banner and proclaim it; / keep nothing back, but say, / 'Babylon will be captured.' " Babylon stands for the evil, idol-worshiping kingdoms in the Bible. Because there was active idol worship in St. Croix, Curt and his teammates began to feel that they were indeed on a holy mission. This banner would be a wordless proclamation to those who loved the Lord and to those who stood against him that Jesus was staking his claim over the island.

Before long the banner became a reality. Everyone was ready to move. I have an awesome photograph of four young missionaries walking, sunburned and smiling, with Curt in the middle. Lifted high above their heads is a huge, colorful satin banner, notifying any and all enemies of the Lord that this island was under new management. How I treasure that photograph!

Dear Heavenly Father, thank you that you still speak to us. If we will listen, we will hear you giving us work to do in your world. We choose to carve out times of quiet in which we can tune in to your voice as you show us your will. Help us to hear you and to act on your instructions. Amen.

34

God's Rescue Operation

*We do not know what to do, but our eyes
are upon you.*

2 Chronicles 20:12

Being a writer calls me into intimate relationships with people I have never met. You
are one of those people. Though I can't see
the scenery outside your window or the
heartbreak inside your heart, I still feel that I
know you very well. I know that you
struggle. You suffer. You have joy and pain
— challenging and rewarding relationships.
Sometimes you are filled with boldness and
confidence and sometimes you are paralyzed
by indecision and fear.

How can I claim to know you so intimately? Because we are both members of
the human race and we go through the
same kinds of things. We both have a desperate need for God.

That's why in difficult times we can pray
as Jehoshaphat did in 2 Chronicles 20:12:
"We do not know what to do, but our eyes
are on you." That prayer of powerlessness

releases all of God's power into our situation. Then we can hear these words:

Don't be afraid! Don't be paralyzed by this mighty army! For the battle is not yours, but God's. . . . Take your places; stand quietly and see the incredible rescue operation God will perform for you. . . . Go out there tomorrow, for the Lord is with you." (2 Chron. 20:15, 17 TLB)

What good news this is for us! In fact this message has so empowered me that I want to print it on colorful leaflets and have them dropped by the thousands into the hearts of believers everywhere.

What is the universal good news in 2 Chronicles 20? We don't have to struggle in order to figure out the answers to all our problems. In fact exactly the opposite is true. Our part is to stop trying to do it our way and let God be God. Let's look at how that works.

Our part in a crisis is:

- to surrender our will and our way to God in prayer.
- to keep our eyes focused on him.
- to stand still and listen to him.
- to choose not to be afraid or discouraged.

- to show up and see what God will do.

Notice that none of these steps is aggressive. None of them makes us the hero of the story. Instead, each of them calls for us to watch, to wait, to listen for God's will and to trust his ability to perform on our behalf.

But it's also important to note that we don't stay in bed with the pillow over our heads. We get up, we show up, we stand up, we look up, we listen up, and we follow up! In every way we can, we participate as his children.

O Father, increase our faith so we can put everything in your hands. Increase our courage to believe in your rescue operation. Help us release our lives and problems to you. Amen.

35

How Wide and Long and High and Deep

[I pray] that Christ may dwell in your hearts through faith. And I pray that you, being rooted and established in love, may have power, together with all the saints, to grasp how wide and long and high and deep is the love of Christ, and to know this love that surpasses knowledge — that you may be filled to the measure of all the fullness of God.

Ephesians 3:17–19

There is something huge and powerful going on in these three verses — so much so, in fact, that Paul was wrestling with a sense of frustration.

To the people of Ephesus (and to us, the Christians who have followed behind them) he was saying, "Listen! You're going to need every ounce of faith you've got to wrap your mind around what I'm about to tell you. You're going to have to open the door of your hearts as wide as they will possibly go and invite Jesus to move in —

124

lock, stock, and barrel — or you're going to miss it.

"Get rooted and grounded, church," he was saying. "Get established, entrenched, embedded, and fixed in the love of Jesus Christ. Get excited! Because unless you do, you're never going to get it. You're never going to have the power to experience him fully."

How can we understand what is beyond our ability to understand? How can we know the love that surpasses our knowledge? This love is wider and longer and higher and deeper than our comprehension.

This is the love that stoops to conquer. This is the love that reaches to redeem. This is the center and the soul of the Father who revealed himself in the life of the Son as he walked among the men and women of earth, holding children on his lap, teaching the lessons of the kingdom, healing the physical and emotional wounds of those who followed him.

Look at him. Let the eyes of your faith rest on the one who was willing to leave crowns and thrones and angels' praises to become a baby laid on straw. Look at him, the one who bowed to be baptized though he had never sinned. Look at him, the one who faced his own accusers, wordlessly accepting their sentence on his life; the one who bore abuse and torture, who bled and finally died so that we could live to laugh and love and be reconciled to his Father.

All that we need to know of God's amazing love — his deep and long and high and wide love for us — we will find in his Son.

Look at his Son. Look at your Savior. Open your heart and you will be filled to all the measure of the fullness with the wonder and the power of God.

Oh, Father, we praise you for giving us a love so enormous it is unknowable. Reveal your identity to us more and more each day. We invite the presence and the power of your Son to move in. Touch us and change us and heal us as we dwell daily in you. Amen.

36

Forty Thousand Testimonies

Great is your faithfulness.
                    Lamentations 3:23

Spike was tired — truly tired. He had driven with our son Andy in his ten-year-old Toyota truck five hours to Atlanta to attend a Promise Keepers conference. The traffic had been something we small-town dwellers can fathom only in our worst nightmares.

The conference they were attending was rewarding but activity-packed with speakers, small groups, and times of worship. But perhaps the most draining part of the three-day gathering for my introverted husband was being packed sardine-style into a mammoth stadium with nearly forty thousand men. When he climbed the ramps with Andy to their seats high in the stadium, he admitted to God and to himself his enormous sense of fatigue.

Then, as they took their seats, the worship leader began very quietly to sing a familiar hymn a capella. His eyes were closed; his palms were open as though he expected something precious to be placed in them. He lifted his rich baritone voice toward heaven and the words floated out across the heads of the men.

"Great is thy faithfulness," O God my
    Father,
There is no shadow of turning with
    Thee;
Thou changest not, Thy compassions,
    they fail not;
As Thou hast been Thou forever wilt
    be.

Gradually, like the wind blowing through a field of wheat, one and two and ten and twenty at a time, forty thousand men began to rise to their feet. They began to lift their hearts and hands and voices in prayer and praise. And it became clear that not only did these men know the song, they knew the one to whom they were singing. And they worshiped him for his steady grace in their lives.

Spike said that all around him he was aware that each man had an inner and invisible story of God's faithfulness. Though he couldn't see or hear those testimonies, he could feel them in the invisible heartbeat of that prayer-filled moment. Each man represented a life that God had touched and changed and rescued.

Spike thought of God's faithfulness in our own desperate moment of need. He said that he could see in his mind's eye the day we brought our eighteen-year-old son to enroll him in a drug treatment center. Our sense of powerlessness and failure had been palpable.

But then Spike said he turned his head slightly to see that same son worshiping beside him, now clean and sober for twelve years, now a Christian, a husband, a father, a friend, and Spike was overwhelmed with a gratitude that literally took the song from his throat and sent tears coursing down his cheeks. He could only praise God.

Father, you are unchanging. There is no shadow of turning in you. Teach us to depend on you, to breathe in the oxygen of your goodness. We love you, Lord.

37

A Prayer for Boldness

Enable your servants to speak your word with great boldness. Stretch out your hand to heal and perform miraculous signs and wonders through the name of your holy servant Jesus.

Acts 4:29–30

If we ever thought that we had to speak for God out of our fleshly wisdom, how intimidated we would feel. If we ever thought that it was totally up to us to do God's work from our human resources, how inadequate we would feel. But we know that God has promised to supply us with the boldness we require through his power. Acts 4:29–30 is a prayer in which the disciples asked God for courage, and Acts 4:31 tells us, "After they prayed, the place where they were meeting was shaken. And they were all filled with the Holy Spirit and spoke the word of God boldly."

Years ago I heard author Henri Nouwen share a personal parable that paints a picture of the trust we can place in God's willingness and power to answer our prayer for boldness. Nouwen had taken his eighty-eight-year-old father to the circus in Germany. Though the circus tent was full of wild and colorful sights, Henri was bored — until the trapeze artists came out. Then he watched spellbound.

In fact Henri was so fascinated, he decided to go back and see if he could speak to those high-flying acrobats after the show. As Henri questioned the head of the family of trapeze artists about the amazing skill he had acquired, the seasoned performer revealed a secret Henri had never suspected.

"You know," he said, "since I am the main flyer in the act and I can do triple flips, I get all the applause. But I'll tell you a secret, Henri. I'm not the hero. The real hero is the catcher. One of the greatest mistakes I could make in the air would be to try to catch the catcher. If I moved my arms around or tried to grab for him, we'd miss the catch. I just have to do my triple and put my arms out and trust that he will catch me. And when I trust, he always does."

Nouwen made the analogy that we have many "triples" to do in our lives, many daily calls for courage. Many of us juggle the responsibilities of holding down jobs and raising families. Others of us carry the weight of everyday work responsibilities and decision-making on our own. Apart from God there is a good chance we could "miss the catch." But we are not the heroes of our own stories. God is the Hero who sent his Son to walk among us. God is the Hero who sends his Spirit to live through us, giving us the wisdom and bravery we need. God is the Hero who will catch us if we will but trust.

Lord my Hero, I put my arms out to you, trusting you to catch me, believing you will uphold me in all things. Empower me and give me boldness to speak and act for you. Amen.

38

Getting on Our Knees

I will obey your decrees;
do not utterly forsake me.

Psalm 119:8

When Toni and her husband were trans-
ferred to South Carolina, she was not a
happy camper. She would be leaving the
friendships she depended on, the church she
loved, and the town in which she had grown
up.

Her new area in South Carolina was
blessed with natural beauty, her new home
was roomy and picturesque, and there
were friendly people waiting to embrace
her. But Toni wasn't going to give in that
easily. She was pouting.

What did God think he was doing,
moving her out of civilization into the
middle of nowhere? How was he going to
use her in this strange place? There were
no opportunities for her to play her French
horn here, no cultural advantages anywhere nearby.

God just let Toni pout herself into a regular funk until she was willing to give up her pity party! Finally one day she opened her eyes and realized what she was doing. That was when she got on her knees.

"God," she prayed, "I've wasted so much time on self-pity. Please forgive me. I can't do this on my own. I need you so much. Show me what to do, Lord. Whatever it is, I'll do it."

Something heavy lifted from her spirit right then. She felt a sense of joy! She was following the Lord again. Her life was his adventure, not her ego trip.

The first thing Toni heard the Lord telling her to do was to open a tearoom.

"A tearoom?" she questioned. "But I can't even cook!"

"Just trust me," he said.

So Toni, with the help of several other ladies in her husband's congregation, began preparing a delicious and beautifully served luncheon after church every Sunday. All of the town's denominations began to be attracted to The Parish House, as the tearoom was called. In fact, it became a meeting place for the whole town.

The next message she got from God involved putting on concerts for people in the little town. She was surprised to find that there were several other musicians who missed using their gifts on the piano, violin, viola, and Toni herself on the French horn.

I was in awe when she sent me a video of their first performance. Not only classical pieces, but also worship choruses and hymns were on the program. God was honored as these musicians brought their talents and their faith together.

Why do we doubt that God longs to use whoever we are wherever we are if only we will yield to him? He's waiting only for a prayerful surrender.

Father God, thank you for the adventure you have in store for us. Help us not to lose a minute insisting on our own way. We choose to follow you — totally! In Jesus' name, amen.

39

Life-Changing Love

Your love, O LORD, reaches to the heavens,
your faithfulness to the skies.

Psalm 36:5

I have heard it said that if we ever got a true glimpse of God's powerful, all-encompassing love, it would change everything in our lives — everything, in fact, on the face of the planet.

Drinking and drugging would gradually disappear as people began to feel the steadying hand of God's grace on their shoulders. There would be no more insomnia, for we would curl up in our loving Father's arms each night and rest soundly until morning. Madison Avenue advertisers would watch their profits drop as consumers released their need for all the hyped-up hoopla they had been brainwashed into seeing as standard equipment for happiness.

Compulsive eating, compulsive shopping, compulsive gambling would become things of the past. The crime rate would drop. Bitterness and hatred would decrease. Forgiveness and love would increase. Families would begin to be healed. And the world would follow in kind.

Of course that sounds like an outlandish claim. But to the extent that we pray for God's love to invade our small corner of the world, an amazing change really does take place. Think now of times you have come face-to-face with his love and faithfulness through the people in your life. How much has that meant to you?

I think of my mom, who always had time to read to us as children. We would all pile up in bed with her, and she would share the treasured tales of children's literature that she loved so well. I can still see her face as she acted out all the parts.

I think of my mother-in-law, Marjie, who adopted me into the Cloninger clan unreservedly. We had a Naomi-and-Ruth relationship until the day she died.

I think of Jacque, who always makes me laugh and always shares my tears; of Pris, who is never too busy for me; and of Lisa, who has spent hours in prayer for me.

And I think of my dad, who always speaks life-changing words of blessing over me. Only last week I called him. "Daddy, this is Claire," I said loudly, trying to get past his deafness.

"Claire, my baby," he said. "I've been thinking about you all day. Thinking about how proud I am of you. You've made such a good life for your family and you've raised such fine children."

I was suddenly quiet. Why had I called him? My heart was so flooded with love and grace, I couldn't even remember.

Oh, Father, we thank you for your life-changing love and the ways that it invades our hearts through the love of other people. Fill us with your Holy Spirit and empower us to love others for you. In Jesus' name, amen.

40

Following the Treasure Map

*You have made known to me the path of
life;*
you will fill me with joy in your presence,
with eternal pleasures at your right hand.
Psalm 16:11

Our little granddaughter, three-year-old
Caroline, has a fairly irresistible way of requesting what she wants from the adults in
her life. Recently while with her other grandmother she posed this question: "I'm thirsty,
Momlee. What are my options?"

"Well," her Momlee replied, trying not
to laugh, "you may have milk, water, or
lemonade."

Caroline was thoughtful for a minute before speaking. "You know," she said, "root
beer is always a good option."

How often we are like Caroline with our
heavenly Father. We pray fervently for
him to show us his will. We ask him to
make our choices clear. And then when he
answers our prayers in no uncertain
terms, we try to slip in a suggestion that is

more to our liking.

God has revealed our options to us in his Word. To find the joy of his presence is to exercise the gift of prayer. It is to follow his will and walk the obedient path.

If you have temporarily lost your joy, ask the Lord to show you the point at which you may have left the path of obedience and turned from his presence. Think of it as a map — a treasure map — and ask him to lead you back to the place and the time when you may have deserted your prayer life. There will be no joy apart from communion with him, and no communion without the practice of prayer. I recall one stressful time in my own life when I rushed to finish writing a book about having a close, personal relationship with the Lord. I got so busy writing about it, I let my actual practice of that relationship lapse. The words of my own manuscript convicted me. My book would never ring true if it did not grow out of my own prayer life.

Can you think of a time when you turned away? Was it the time you stopped bringing the Lord your heart in simple morning devotionals?

Was it the time when you stopped singing those little worship songs as you rode around in your car?

Was it a time that you stopped investing your heart in a prayerful study of his Word?

Or maybe it was a time when you stopped interceding for friends or family members who needed daily prayer.

These things are not on God's giant to-do list in the sky. He's not keeping score on you. He merely wants you to know his joy, and only prayer can keep your spiritual "pipeline" unclogged so that he can pour out into your life the flood of gladness and blessings he has for you, his child.

Lord Jesus, thank you that it is your desire to give us joy. Help me to hear you clearly as you draw me into daily prayer. Keep my feet on the way of obedience so that I may walk in accordance with your will. Amen.

41

It Gets Better Than This!

Amen. Come, Lord Jesus.
Revelation 22:20

In a recent movie, *As Good as It Gets*, a man named Melvin, played by Jack Nicholson, exits his psychiatrist's office into a room where several other patients are waiting. With a sardonic look on his face Melvin says to them, "What if this is as good as it gets?"

Many people live with Melvin's long-term diagnosis of life. With no hope of heaven, they believe that life as they now know it is all there is.

Journalist Peggy Noonan has said:

We are the first generation of man that actually expected to find happiness here on earth, and our search for it has caused such unhappiness. The reason: If you do not believe in another, higher world, if you believe only in the flat material world around you, if you believe that this is your only chance at happiness . . . then you are not disappointed when the world does not give you a good measure of its riches, you are despairing.[1]

What Jesus holds out to us is real and it is eternal. It has nothing to do with this flat, material world. It has nothing to do with what the stock market is doing today. It is not affected by headlines or wars or crimes or scandals. It has everything to do with the Lord's promise of a glorious life that gets better than this.

"Behold, I am coming soon!" said Jesus to John in the Book of Revelation.

"My reward is with me, and I will give to everyone according to what he has done. I am the Alpha and the Omega, the First and the Last, the Beginning and the End.

"Blessed are those who wash their robes, that they may have the right to the tree of life and may go through the gates into the city.

". . . I, Jesus, have sent my angel to give you this testimony for the churches. I am the Root and the Offspring of David, and the bright Morning Star."

The Spirit and the bride say, "Come!" And let him who hears say, "Come!" Whoever is thirsty, let him come; and whoever wishes, let him take the free gift of the water of life.

(Revelation 22:12–14, 16–17)

To this beautiful invitation to eternal life the apostle John breathed a very short prayer. "Amen," he said, which means "so be it." Then, "Come, Lord Jesus." This is a prayer of belief in the one who is coming, and relief that the time is near.

Let us pray along with John, and then get ready, brothers and sisters. It gets better than this!

Lord Jesus, thank you for your beautiful invitation to share eternity with you. Help us to enjoy the beauty of this world while we're in it but always to keep heaven in our hearts. Amen.

42

It Is Finished

Jesus said, "It is finished." With that, he bowed his head and gave up his spirit.

John 19:30

Our Savior spoke his last prayer to his Father from the cross. He knew that his work was done. Everything that God had commissioned him to carry out he had completed.

Looking at our Lord's life from an earthly perspective, some find it hard to see it as one of great accomplishment. It looks inglorious, to say the least.

- He who had stood at God's right hand left the glory of his heavenly body to take on the frailty of a human body.
- He who had cocreated a universe with his heavenly Father spent his days patiently learning carpentry from his earthly father.
- He who had known the Almighty from before the foundation of time humbly "learned" of him as a boy in the temple and worshiped him there as a man.

- He who could have used his divine powers to trump the enemy's wilderness temptations endured them instead in the flesh.
- He who had spent his time in the company of saints and angels embraced the friendship of fishermen, tax collectors, prostitutes, and children.
- And men made him whom the heavenly host had worshiped and adored a spectacle and a mockery before the crowds who stood before the cross. They captured and questioned him, beat him until his back was raw, then robed him in a "royal mantle." Men scorned him, spat upon him, crowned him with thorns, and made him carry his own cross down a long, unrelenting road. He took nails in his hands and feet while his own blood streamed into his eyes. He spent three hours in the blistering sun, gasping for a breath. And worst of all, he felt as though his Father had turned away.

What was he thinking as he breathed those final words, "It is finished"? Was he aware of the victory? Did he feel grateful that he was going to his Father? How much did he understand?

I don't know. I know only that I praise

him now for staying the course and finishing his race — for suffering and bleeding and dying for me. And as I hear his final prayer in my heart I praise him that when my life is over, because of his sacrifice, I will be able to stand before his Father with joy.

Thank you, Father, for the cross, for the shed blood of my Savior, and for your perfect plan of salvation. Thank you for seeking me when I was hiding and forgiving me the minute I repented. Thank you that there will be a time for me when I am able to pray, as Jesus did, "It is finished." May I then find my place in your perfect kingdom. Amen.

43

Open the Eyes of Our Hearts

*I pray also that the eyes of your heart may
be enlightened in order that you may know
the hope to which he has called you.*

Ephesians 1:18

Every now and then a new song flows like
water into the thirsty church, crossing de-
nominational lines, making its way into the
hearts of God's people. Paul Baloche wrote
one such song when he composed "Open
the Eyes of My Heart." I heard him say in a
seminar that he was not even trying to write
a song the day he wrote it. He was simply
worshiping God, singing a paraphrase of
Ephesians 1:18.

So many of us live in a world of rush and
stress. How we need moments of worship
in which we stop and focus our spiritual
eyes on Jesus. Scripture tells us to "seek
the LORD and His strength; / seek His face
continually" (1 Chron. 16:11 NASB). "My
eyes are continually toward the LORD,"
said the psalmist, "for He will pluck my
feet out of the net" (Ps. 25:15 NASB).

When we feel that a snare of commitments, hurry, and busyness has trapped us, we can open the eyes of our hearts to Jesus. As we do, the confusion clears. We see that we need not do a hundred things or fifty things or even ten; we need do only one: obey him, one small task at a time. When we see it, we suddenly find the flower of peace blooming in the field of frustration. We find the gentle flow of order springing up in the desert of chaos.

What happens when we are vulnerable enough to come to the Lord in prayer, seeking him with open eyes? Exactly what gets transformed when we focus willing hearts on him? He changes our whole perspective.

He helps us discern between what we have and what we need.

He teaches us to focus our lives on one person, one moment, and one need at a time.

He gives us eyes to see the beauty and the value in each person with whom we spend time.

He lets us peel away the irritations in our lives and look at the hidden joy beneath them — the things for which we can be thankful.

In short, he lets us see life as the treasure that it is.

It is so easy to waste precious moments with the futilities and letdowns of life when just changing the direction of our glance — just looking to the Lord and giving him our praise — will bring our hearts to a whole new place.

Oh, Lord, I want to see you in every part of my life. Don't let me waste a single moment. Thank you for the treasures of life — my friends, my family, my work, my faith. You have filled my life with beauty. Open the eyes of my heart. Amen.

44

Four Radical Evangelists

I said to the LORD, "You are my Lord. . . ."
As for the saints who are in the land,
they are the glorious ones in whom
is all my delight.

Psalm 16:2–3

Spike and I were on the way home from our midweek church service when we realized we had missed dinner. "Let's stop at Arby's," he suggested.

I should tell you our church is in a pretty rough part of town, and it was late. But I swallowed any fear I had about the neighborhood and agreed. I was hungry.

As we entered the restaurant, I was relieved to see only one little old lady sipping tea in the corner. So we put in our order for beef with cheese and a double order of curly fries.

That's when they walked in: four motorcycle types you wouldn't want to meet in a dark alley. They wore black sleeveless T-shirts, leather cowboy hats, earrings, and wall-to-wall tattoos. Their hair was long and stringy. One had a long blonde pigtail. And they were walking in our direction.

"Don't get freaked," Spike said to me.

"They've probably got guns — or knives. Oh, God, help us," I prayed under my breath.

The biggest of them reached in his pocket and pulled something out. I steeled myself for the worst.

It was a pocket-sized New Testament. In his gentle Southern accent he got right down to business. "Have you folks accepted Jesus Christ as your personal Lord and Savior?" he asked.

We were stunned and a little speechless at first. "We sure have," we finally answered.

"Well, that's good to hear!" he said. "That means we're brothers and sisters in the Lord."

"Praise God," said Spike.

"Where do you folks worship?" asked our new friend.

"At Christ Church," I answered, gesturing toward the bay.

"Do you know Andy Cloninger?" asked the shortest of them. "He worships there."

We couldn't help but laugh. "Oh, yes," we answered. "We've known Andy for a long time. We're his parents."

"No kidding," said the one with the pig-tail. "Andy plays guitar for us when we do street ministry. He's way cool."

We had to agree.

We had a great time of fellowship that night at Arby's with these four radical evangelists. We heard about their street ministry and how many had been saved that week. I realized that these were "the saints who are in the land" — the ones in whom David delighted in Psalm 16.

"Lord," I prayed, "forgive me for being such a narrow-minded Pharisee. These guys are on the front lines of the battle. There is so much I can learn from them. Open my eyes and my heart to see and intercede for the whole family of God."

Oh, Father, thank you for continuing to stretch me, for continuing to put me in uncomfortable situations in which I can see your face and learn more of you. I love you, Lord! Amen.

45

Perfect Love on an Imperfect Planet

*Lord! Help! Godly men are fast disap-
pearing. Where in all the world can de-
pendable men be found? Everyone deceives
and flatters and lies.*

Psalm 12:1–2 TLB

In this plaintive prayer David had lost his
faith in humankind. He was crying out for a
friend, casting his eyes about for one true-
hearted person. Face-to-face, gaze to gaze,
where is the one who will not flatter or lie?
The one who will not con or swindle? The
one who will deal evenly and honestly?

Have you ever felt like this? During an
election, for instance, have you ever felt
that each politician was pointing the ac-
cusing finger at his opponent while self-
righteously puffing out his own chest as
though he were humanity's answer?

During the Wall Street scandals of 2002,
were you stunned to see businesspeople
you had thought were on the up-and-up
sinking to new lows in business ethics?

Or more importantly, have you ever

needed just one caring friend or loved one who would hear you and help you: a friend who would invest honest input — no backing up, no cover-up, just plain talk, lovingly stated — into your life?

All around us people are needing that kind of friend: the friend with ample time for love and zero tolerance for lies — not even little white ones. The friend whose life reveals the qualities of love that Paul wrote about in 1 Corinthians 13: patience, kindness, a lack of jealousy, envy, boastfulness, or pride.

Everything else in this world will disappear. Even God's great spiritual gifts will dissolve into mist and lift like a vapor, but love like this will last — strong and sure and powerful.

When I was a child, my thoughts were childlike. Now that I'm an adult, God is giving me grown-up thoughts. When I was a child I longed for a perfect friend, just as David did. But God is showing me now that all along Jesus was the perfect friend for whom I had longed. All along my yearning for a perfect relationship was a desire for a love relationship with him.

If I look to human beings, I'm destined to be let down. Everyone from the most crooked politician to the closest human friend will fall short when compared to the perfect one for whom my heart was designed. So the Lord is whispering to me today to stop looking in all the wrong faces for perfect love, and to look to his Son.

Lord God, I thank you that you have set a longing for pure love in my heart, and all along you have planned to fulfill that longing with your own friendship. I come to you today, empty and needy, and I ask you to be the friend I've always needed. Fill me with the love my heart desires and requires. Amen.

46

Praise Like Incense

May my prayer be set before you like incense.

Psalm 141:2

How can we describe the experience of worship? In some ways it is like the relationship between the climber and the mountain. The climber stands in awe of and beholds what he could never create. And yet there is an insatiable hunger within him to meet and experience the mountain.

Or perhaps the relationship is more like that of singer and song. What is a song, really? A miracle of notes and words strung together on some lovely line of reason. (Or lack of reason.) And yet the voice is pulled by an outer force and an inner yearning to surf the currents of the melody; to be lifted out of its boundaries into the heavenlies of the heart.

Must we know God to worship him? It helps, though I believe many of us glimpse his reality before we ever meet him, and we worship. He is always with us, trying to get our attention — showing off with his sunsets and his butterflies, throwing some line of dialogue into our daily conversation to draw the heart and intrigue the spirit.

He's there in the eyes of a child, in the laughter of a friend. Wherever people love people and help and care, he is there. He's there when we choose to come into his presence. He's the hand of comfort that touches us in grief and the surprising joy that comes at unbidden moments.

All These and More

He's all we've heard and read of him
The phrases and the words,
The Psalms and hymns and awe-filled songs
The lovely, liquid lines of verse,
The patriarchs, the Pentateuch,
The Proverbs and Epistles,
Creation and captivity,
The hill that led to Calvary,
The crown of thorns, the cross, the nails,
The suffering, the dying King
The spear that drew the crimson blood
The anguished words, "My God, my God"
That echoed through a hell of pain
The battered body quietly laid

Within a borrowed burial grave.
The boulder and the weeping friends,
The silent sound of love's "amen"
Then when it seemed to end too soon
The open door, the empty tomb!

We see by faith and not by sight
That blurred and bright reality.
We see the one we've never met,
And trust the one we've never seen.
Rock solid and intractable.
Transient and full of grace.
Through him we glimpse eternity
And lift the incense of our praise
And "Holy" blends with holiness
"Forever" touched by fingertips
Beyond all sensibility
We worship him alone
Holy, holy, holy to the Lamb upon the
throne.

Claire Cloninger

*Holy, holy, holy, Lord! How good you are to
create us for a relationship with you and then to
pursue us relentlessly until we finally turn and
see you there! May your lungs be filled with the
incense of our worship all day long. We want to
know you more, our God and our King, our All
in all. Amen.*

47

Practicing His Presence

*Blessed are those who have learned to
    acclaim you,
who walk in the light of your presence,
    O Lord.*

Psalm 89:15

As a writer I'm always fascinated by what
makes a book last. Of the dozen or so that
I've written, several are already out of print.
How I grieved for those little books. They
died so young!

One of my favorite books, *The Practice
of the Presence of God*, is more than five
hundred years old! Its author was a six-
teenth-century monk named Brother
Lawrence. Brother Lawrence was not a religious leader or theologian. He was a
simple man who worked in the kitchen of
a monastery. He never intended to write a
book. He just wrote letters to his friends,
telling them about his friendship with his
wonderful Savior, Jesus Christ. But people
gathered those letters and had them
bound into a book. And that book has

outlasted thousands of others.

It's not hard to figure why once you read it. Brother Lawrence's book expresses one of the most profound secrets of the faith. He learned to remind himself all day long that he was in God's presence.

This is such a simple secret that we often discount it. But it has transformed untold lives. It has the power to change any day from chaotic to peaceful, from depressing to joyful, from boring to exciting. Just knowing the Lord is present changes everything.

My brother Charlie is a wonderful poet. When his daughter Meg was three years old he wrote a poem entitled "A Walk with My Small Daughter." In the poem little Meg would bound out ahead of Charlie, gathering the treasures of her day, and return to Charlie so that he could help her identify them.

"What is it, Papa?" she would ask. "Rock . . . leaf . . . feather," she would repeat after him as he helped her understand her world.

I love this picture because it shows what our relationship with God can and should be. We can bound out ahead of him in the spontaneity of an unguarded moment, safe in the security of his loving presence. His eyes are on us. And we can trust that he is listening to our words. We don't have to shout. We don't have to use four-syllable theological words. A three-year-old's rhetoric suits him fine.

Brother Lawrence described his prayer life as "a silent and secret conversation of my soul with God." We, too, can enjoy God like this. In his presence we are treasured and watched over as he helps us to understand and celebrate every step along the way.

Dear Lord, simplify my heart. I come to you as a little child. Wherever I am today, it's because you put me here. Teach me to listen for your words, follow your ways, and most of all, Lord, to practice your presence. Amen.

48

Praise to the One Who Strengthens Us

May our Lord Jesus Christ . . . encourage your hearts and strengthen you in every good deed and word.
2 Thessalonians 2:16–17

When Jesus first found several of his disciples they were working by the Sea of Galilee. After hard days of fishing, they probably smelled of perspiration and fish scales. Upon returning to shore, they likely had tackled the job of cleaning fish first, then occupied themselves with mending their nets.

When reading a commentary on 2 Thessalonians I was fascinated to find that the phrase "restoring and strengthening" had the same meaning as "the mending of nets." I loved that.

I know I need God's restoration when I've been out in the thick of his work. Don't you? I need him to mend my nets when they are torn by fatigue, low self-esteem, or envy. I need him to strengthen me and shore me up, to restore me and give me renewed faith and confidence. I need him to overhaul every spiritual thing about me. I cannot be useful when my nets are torn and in need of repair.

Our enemy is determined to destroy the nets with which we do the work of the kingdom. He is out to see that we suffer and become useless in our fight against all that is evil.

But when we are at our lowest, we discover that the God of all grace is on our side. He who has called us to his eternal glory in his Son Jesus Christ has made it clear that our suffering in the spiritual battle will not go on forever and it will not be in vain. What's more, after we have suffered a little while, he will be the one who restores us (mends our nets). He will give us encouragement and hope. He will strengthen us in every good deed and make us firm and steadfast in the fight (1 Pet. 5:10).

How can we not lift a prayer of praise and thanksgiving to the God of all grace who goes with us into the fight, and who calls us to his own eternal glory in his Son? How can we not say of our God, "To him be the power for ever and ever. Amen"?

Oh, Father, you are always coming to my de-

fense. I worship you for that. You truly are the God of all grace. Your mercies surround me. You call me to you and I come joyfully. You call me to your glory. You repair my nets and steady my feet. To you be all praise and thanksgiving forever and ever. Amen.

49

A Prayer from an Honest Heart

Hear, O LORD, my righteous plea; listen to
my cry.
Give ear to my prayer —
it does not rise from deceitful lips.
May my vindication come from you;
may your eyes see what is right.
Though you probe my heart and examine
*   me at night,*
though you test me, you will find nothing;
I have resolved that my mouth will not sin.

Psalm 17:1–3

How many of us would have the audacity to
stride into God's presence one morning,
presenting ourselves to him as "totally righteous"? The moment we'd try to make such
a claim we'd be puffed up with pride and our
so-called righteousness would go up in
smoke. The moment we'd try to present ourselves as "totally honest" we'd already have
lied. Nobody's totally honest. So where did
David get off making such an audacious
claim to the Lord in this prayer?

The righteousness he claimed was not

what we might imagine. Unlike our straight-laced, stiff-collared puritanical stereotype, David was not claiming a total lack of sin. He was not parading the false piety of the "religious" crowd.

Instead, David's kind of righteousness meant being right with God, having a reconciled relationship with him, shooting straight with him, and not trying to sound pious when God knew he wasn't. And it meant giving God free access to his heart.

And what of David's kind of honesty? David's heart was an open book before God. He had given up any attempt at deceit. He longed for a friendship with the Father.

Now, with our terms redefined, let's try paraphrasing David's prayer:

O Lord, it's me again. I don't want to hide from you. I need you so much. That's why I'm here, crying out to you. Please help me. You can see my heart, so you know what's in it. You know that what I'm saying isn't a lie. You're the only one who knows how to straighten out the situation I'm in. Help me, Lord. Take a good look at my motives and my desires. If there's anything false or selfish in me, show it to me so I can confess it. I want to be right with you. I don't want to say or do anything that will cause any harm to anyone else. Help me to be your person in this and every situation, Father.

Do you hear David's words differently now? I believe that God is always looking for the heart that will deal honestly with him — the heart of a person who desires a righteous relationship with him.

Dear Father, help me to want what you want for me — pure motives and an honest heart. I acknowledge that apart from you these things are impossible, so I lift my soul to you in prayer and ask you to have your way in my life. Amen.

50

A Prayer of a Doubter

I do believe; help me overcome my unbelief!
Mark 9:24

Do you have a friend who seems to be a "natural believer"? She glides almost effortlessly over every bump of doubt and disbelief while you seem to be stumbling at every turn. Faith seems to fit your friend like a glove, while on you it feels like someone else's hand-me-downs. Your friend seems to move confidently from victory to victory, while every step you take seems as shaky as an attempt to jump from stone to stone across a river. Your faith-filled friend never seems to have a question, while you are constantly asking God to give you a sign.

Don't be fooled. Everyone doubts at times, and the faith we need we cannot drum up with our own fleshly efforts. Faith is a gift and God alone is the giver of the gift.

When Peter saw Jesus walking to him on the water, he got out of the boat and began to walk toward the Lord. "What faith!" we may say. But as Peter looked around and realized what he was doing, fear took over and he began to sink. Only Jesus was able to give him the faith he needed to stay above his circumstances (see Matt. 14).

Thomas, too, was a doubter who needed faith. Even after his best friends returned from the empty tomb and described what they had seen, Thomas refused to believe. It was only when Jesus appeared to the disciples a week later and invited Thomas to touch his wounds and satisfy his doubts that Thomas found the faith he required.

"Put your finger here; see my hands. Reach out your hand and put it into my side," the Master said. "Stop doubting and believe." And Thomas exclaimed, "My Lord and my God!" (John 20:24–28)

The Bible invites any of us who lack faith to pray in the words of the father who doubted: "I do believe; help me overcome my unbelief."

This is a prayer that God delights to answer. Faith is a gift that he delights to give. God knows what we lack and what we need. He made each of us as we are, and in our character is the raw material he will use to make us who we can become.

Father God, I refuse to doubt and I choose to be-

lieve. Thank you for the good news that you can take every one of my traits and use them to bring you glory. I lift up to you both my strengths and my weaknesses. I surrender myself totally to you. Amen.

51

A Prayer of Meditation

I will meditate on all your works
and consider all your mighty deeds.
Your ways, O God, are holy.
What god is so great as our God?
You are the God who performs miracles;
you display your power among the peoples.
Psalm 77:12–14

Meditating on the mighty deeds, holy works, and powerful miracles of our God enriches our lives. Author Richard J. Foster made a homely analogy relating to meditation, one that I find helpful:

Have you ever watched a cow chew its cud? This unassuming animal will fill its stomach with grass and other food. Then it settles down quietly, and through a process of regurgitation re-works what it has received, slowly moving its mouth in the process. In this way it is able to fully assimilate what it has previously consumed, which is then transformed into rich, creamy milk. So it is with meditative prayer. The truth being meditated upon passes from the mouth into the mind and down into the heart, where through quiet rumination — regurgitation, if you will — it produces in the person praying a loving, faith-filled response.[1]

The more we allow the beauty and truth of God's Word to circulate in our spirits and through our minds — the more we chew the cud of his wisdom, so to speak — the richer the finished product in our lives.

When I meditate on God's Word, first I ask him to lead me to a particular passage. Many times this happens quite naturally as I am reading the Word. A passage of Scripture seems to draw my attention almost as though God was highlighting it.

Once I am at that stopping place, I will write the standout phrase or passage at the top of my journal page and ask the Holy Spirit to teach me what he would have me know. I underline significant words in the passage and then for a time I rest in God's presence. What is he saying to me? Why has he brought me to this place? What is his message? I write it all down.

Beside each significant word I might write other related words that have a particular meaning for me. I might jot down a question or a short thought related to the word or passage. During the week I try to spend quiet times of reflection on these thoughts, not leaving the passage until it has yielded for me the spiritual food that God intended.

I found one such example in a journal entry dated August 30, 2001. I had been struggling with what focus my ministry should take: songwriting, speaking, or writing books? I meditated silently on Proverbs 3:5–6. "Trust in the LORD with all your heart and lean not on your own understanding. In all your ways acknowledge him and he will make your paths straight."

I then wrote out a paraphrase of those verses in my journal: "Lord, I trust you with all my heart. I will not trust my understanding. Lead me and guide me and show me the path I should take."

After another time of quiet, the Lord seemed to give me the following, which answered my question, and I wrote in my journal: "I am a communicator whose gifts of compassion and humor are meant to draw people (mainly, but not exclusively, women) into the warm circle of God's mercy, to bring them to a place of faith and commitment." God seemed to be saying that I need not give up any area of ministry so long as I glorified him.

Oh, Father, teach us to meditate on your Word. Help us not to rush through the riches of what you are saying to us. Slow us down. Let us treasure your company and delight in your conversation. Amen.

52

The Prayer of the Unveiled

To the only wise God be glory forever through Jesus Christ! Amen.

Romans 16:27

This is one of many biblical prayer statements that give God glory. *Glory* tends to be a nebulous term for me. Synonyms such as *magnificence, wonder,* and *brilliance* all fall a little short of the enormity that I envision as God's glory. It's more like a shimmering presence that backlights and highlights all of my life.

I remember a definition of *glory* I wrote down at a Bible study years ago. It said experiencing God's glory was to be "tipped over by his holy presence." His presence *should* tip us over and overwhelm us. The very fact that God has invited us into a relationship with him should send shock waves through our human nature.

In 2 Corinthians 3:18, Paul gave an idea of what hanging out in the holy aura of God's glory would do to us: "And we, who with unveiled faces all reflect the Lord's glory, are being transformed into his likeness with ever-increasing glory, which comes from the Lord, who is the Spirit."

Isn't it true that we become like the people with whom we spend time? What Paul was saying was that God wants this to be true in our relationship with him. If we'll come to him honestly, with unveiled faces, we'll begin to reflect who he is — to be transformed into his likeness as his glory begins to rub off on us.

Why, then, doesn't this transaction take place any more readily than it does? I believe it's because so many of us have become experts at veiling what is really going on. We hide our feelings and thoughts; we disguise our pain and our anger until what we are really bringing God when we come into his presence is little more than a spiritual masquerade. How can we reflect him when we stand before him spiritually covered?

Coming before God honestly in prayer is the first step in allowing him to change us. The confession of any wrong attitudes (anger or jealousy, covetousness or pride) is next. By asking him to shine the light of his holiness into the veiled places in our hearts, revealing to us what needs to be changed, we can begin again to reflect his glory. And finally, standing transparently in the light of who he is, we are able to allow the clear face of who we are to be transformed by his ever-increasing glory.

Father, forgive me when I try to hide, for I know that there is no hiding from your mercy. Forgive me when I try to turn away from the glory that has the amazing power to transform me. Give me the courage to come before you unmasked. I want to be all that you have designed me to be. Work in my life. Amen.

53

A Prayer for Wisdom

I thank and praise you, O God of my
  fathers:
You have given me wisdom and power,
you have made known to me
what we asked of you.

Daniel 2:23

When my son Andy and his wife Jenni were
asked to be youth pastors at Christ Church
in Mobile, they felt they were standing on
shaky ground.

They had some experience as Young Life
leaders and camp counselors. But when
they talked to other youth pastors in the
area they always came away feeling under-
qualified. Why? They had not had any
formal training or schooling in the field.

Still they felt God drawing their hearts
to the job. So they determined to pray for
wisdom as they made their decision. What
would God have them do?

As they began to pray and listen to God,
Andy heard him saying, "How educated
was Peter? Or James or John? And yet they

answered my call. What makes you different? Are you putting formal education above my right to lead you into my own plans?"

"Lord, if you want us to do this, you'll have to show us how to lead these kids," they prayed.

Then God gave Andy and Jenni his formula for working with the youth: "Let us love one another, for love comes from God. Everyone who loves has been born of God and knows God" (1 John 4:7). They decided that this was the best education they could have: to be born of him and to know him.

"Don't worry about exactly how you'll do it," God seemed to be saying. "Just trust me. As long as you let them know that you love them and I love them, you'll be fulfilling my commission and I will work through you."

So Andy and Jenni accepted the job and began to decorate the big empty room that the church designated as the youths'. They scrubbed floors and painted in wild colors. They brought in cast-off sofas and chairs. They spread out worn rugs and put down big comfortable cushions. They gathered a mismatched conglomeration of tables and lamps, and stocked a couple of second-hand refrigerators with Cokes and Dr Peppers and pitchers of iced tea.

When the work was done, they looked around at what God had given them to work with. It didn't seem like much. But they knew it would be more than enough.

And regardless of what they taught or did every Sunday night, they would hug the kids when they arrived and when they were leaving. "I love you," they would say, "and God loves you."

That was the good news that turned the tide for the youth of Christ Church. Many of them accepted Christ for the first time that year. Others recommitted their lives. Still others who had been lukewarm about their faith got fired up. The kids began to pray for each other. One young man even led his parents to the Lord. The group ministered on mission trips both in the States and in foreign countries.

During the four years that Andy and Jenni worked with the youth they had many opportunities to discover what an amazing difference God can make when we surrender our hearts to him in prayer and follow his lead.

Praise you, Lord, for providing us with wisdom.

Thank you for what you can do when we are willing to depend on you. Thank you that when we have been born of you, you work through us! Amen.

54

Nothing Is Too Difficult

Ah, Sovereign LORD, *you have made the heavens and the earth by your great power and outstretched arm. Nothing is too hard for you.*

Jeremiah 32:17

Can't you just picture God stretching out his arm one morning the way we might stretch when we first wake up? Can't you picture him flinging out a universe like we might fling out a handful of sunflower seeds? Suddenly billions of stars and suns and planets and moons are brought into being. How can we fathom such power?

But God has created more than suns and planets and solar systems. He has created us — human beings, the gem of his creation, who, like him, possess the ability to think and feel and reason and love. And he has called us into a love relationship with him. He has invited us to pray to him and has promised to hear us. He wants to communicate!

I remember waiting for a departing flight

in the airport of Tegucigalpa, Honduras, after a mission trip several years ago. It was a hot, noisy, crowded place and I was surrounded by colorfully clad Hondurans all speaking rapidly in Spanish. Possessing virtually no skills in Spanish, I felt totally lost and left out.

Then it occurred to me that our sovereign Lord was listening to every heart in that airport. It was not too difficult for him to hear each of us distinctly though we were "broadcasting" in a great jumble of thoughts, words, languages, and prayers all at the same time.

Though I am only one small person on one small planet in one small solar system, I am not a speck to my Father. I am his daughter. He knows more than my DNA, more than my fingerprints, more than my family background. He knows me. In fact he has known me from before the foundations of the world.

When David considered the fact that God had searched him and known him; had known his sitting and his rising; had perceived his thoughts from afar; was familiar with all his ways, he could only conclude, "Such knowledge is too wonderful for me" (Ps. 139:16).

It may seem too wonderful for you, too.

But it is true. God knows us and loves us. He sent his own Son to earth to seek us out. And he is waiting right now to hear our prayers. There is nothing too small or too large to bring before our Father in heaven. There is nothing he won't hear and help with. There is nothing too difficult for him. Talk to him today!

O Sovereign Lord who created the heavens with your mighty arm, thank you for the mercies that you shower on me. Thank you that you have created me to love you and then drawn me to you. Thank you that instead of keeping me at a distance you have invited me to be a part of your family. I accept your invitation! Amen.

55

The Prayer of the Inner Music

Thanks be to God for his indescribable gift!
2 Cor. 9:15

Years ago I read a quote by Oliver Wendell
Holmes that got my attention. He said,
"Many people go to their graves with their
music still in them."

How sad, I thought at the time. "Lord,
don't let that happen to me. Let not even
one note of music in me remain unwritten
or unsung."

I have worked in Christian music for
twenty-two years. I consider my songwriting a God-given gift. I have written
hundreds of songs. But I know there is
music still in me — music that is as yet unwritten and unsung. It's highly possible
that I have not yet created my best song.
To me that is a pleasurable thought. So
every morning when I talk with the Lord I
ask him to bring forth the unwritten songs
in me.

The longer I walk with the Lord, the
more time I spend in the body of Christ,

the more convinced I am that there is music in each of us. It may not be literal music. But it is a gift that we must bring forth if we are to fulfill our destinies in Christ and give glory to God.

My sister-in-law, Valli, and her husband, Brad, have adopted four children, but their love of children is so strong that it has motivated them to foster more than one hundred others. They often seek out the unadoptable kids, the ones with physical or mental challenges. In their large stone Kentucky farmhouse they love these children back to life. This is Valli and Brad's "music," and it is a beautiful song indeed.

My niece, Julie Salisbery, is graduating this summer from medical school. Her goal is to spend part of every year doing short-term medical mission work in Central and South America. She is ready to do what it takes to "sing this song" of ministry to God's glory.

Our friend Gaston Irby is bursting with the creativity of decorating. He practically dreams the colors and patterns and shapes that make life more beautiful.

On Sunday mornings when Sharissa Mainwaring picks up her violin, I know I'm in for a worship experience. She plays straight from the heart and makes our worship team unique.

I don't know what your inner music is. It may be a warm apple pie shared with a neighbor, coaching a neighborhood basketball team, or letters written to shut-ins. I do know that every gift we offer in love is like a prayer. Every gift we send out into the world is music to our Father's ears.

O Father, I praise you for giving us "songs to sing" that enrich our lives and connect us to your kingdom. Make my life a prayer to you. Bring forth the inner music of my gifts so that they may bring glory to you and be a blessing to others. In Jesus' name, amen.

56

One Small Life

But let all who take refuge in you be glad;
let them ever sing for joy.

Psalm 5:11

Years ago my neighbor Martha asked me to teach her neighborhood Bible study for teenage girls. I was rushed that week and didn't get around to planning ahead of time. So when we gathered, I bowed my head and sent up one of those "Dear God, SOS" kind of prayers.

Just as I looked up from my prayer, my eye landed on a *Life* magazine lying open on the coffee table to an article about a then-current teen heartthrob. I read with interest of the young man's rise to stardom as well as his confession that fame had brought with it new tensions and a tendency to stay isolated from others. He was photographed with his expensive automobiles at his California ranch.

Just a few pages away, I found a second article of interest about Mother Teresa and her ministry to the poor in India. Here was the story of a young girl who left her native Albania motivated by a call to serve God. After becoming a nun and teaching for several years, she was drawn to helping the poor people she saw all around her. She had no master plan and no desire for fame. She merely began to meet the need closest at hand, caring for one destitute or dying person at a time, until within a matter of years, a great international ministry had grown up around her.

When the Nobel Prize committee selected this petite nun to receive its coveted award, no one could have been more surprised than the recipient herself. She had never sought nor anticipated the worldwide acclaim that came to her.

In the article was a close-up photograph of Mother Teresa. Her weathered old face was totally surrendered to the laughter of an unguarded moment. It was an expression of contagious joy.

Here were two stories about two famous people whose lives had influenced the world: one who was committed to making a "big splash" and the other who was content to send out small ripples of love in an ocean of pain; one who was soaking up the rays of the world's spotlight and the other who was reflecting the light of Christ; one who was intent on drawing attention to himself and the other who had chosen to turn her attention to those in need of God's mercy. Which one was happier? Which one had made the world a better place?

The teenage girls and I got into a wonderful discussion about how each of us is given only one small life, and it's up to us to choose how we will use it. I remember at the end of the study a girl named Lori prayed that God would use her life and help her find the kind of joy and fulfillment that Mother Teresa had found.

I have often thought of that discussion and prayed what Lori prayed — that God would deliver my one small life from the wide road of the self-life and keep me on the narrow and joyful path of living for him.

Oh, Father, in you we find our joy. In you our needs are met. You lead us and love us and give us your grace. We praise you, O Lord our God. Amen.

57

Manna and Miracles

In their hunger you gave them bread from heaven and in their thirst you brought them water from the rock.

Nehemiah 9:15

Traveling around the country speaking at women's conferences, I often share the story of how the Lord lifted our son Andy out of the downward spiral of drug addiction. Sometimes Andy accompanies me to lead worship and tell his side of the story.

Because the problem of addiction is such a common one, speaking about it never fails to strike a chord. Everyone in every crowd knows someone who has been touched by the problem of drugs — a child, a sibling, a parent, a friend. Relating our story gives other people hope.

Though this is among our family's most powerful stories of God's healing, it is not the most current. It took place thirteen years ago, and many miracles have occurred since then. God has answered many prayers.

God is constantly working in all of us in

the present tense. He is continually molding us — drawing us into new paths of healing, giving us the life and the power we need to reflect his light.

As Andrew Murray said, "It is not the remembrance of what Jesus has once done to me, but the living experience of what he is *now* to me, that will give me the power to act like Him. His love must be a present reality, the inflowing of a life and power in which I can love like Him."[1]

I believe the present reality about which Andrew Murray spoke is the daily way in which Jesus empowers us to live for him. It is the way he enables us to follow the blueprint of his life, to practice the union and the friendship into which he has called us.

I am grateful to the Lord that he never expects me to live on yesterday's manna. He always gives me a fresh supply. I love the miracles, big and small, he has done in the past, but I also love to tell about the fresh miracles he has delivered and the prayers he has answered.

There's the way he helped me find the car keys just this morning. Wasn't that his grace? Or the extra money in the checking account to send to a missionary couple — wasn't that his mercy? I think also of the way God is growing our children and our grandchildren up in the faith.

May I never take any of these daily mercies for granted. They are the manna and the miracles that fuel my faith.

Oh, Lord, thank you for your present-tense miracles. I don't have to go back five years or ten. You've been here all along, giving me manna and showing me mercy. I love you, Lord. Amen.

58

Gospel in a Nutshell

At that time Jesus, full of joy through the Holy Spirit, said, "I praise you, Father, Lord of heaven and earth, because you have hidden these things from the wise and learned, and revealed them to little children. Yes, Father, for this was your good pleasure."

Luke 10:21

This morning I talked on the phone to my granddaughter Caroline in North Carolina. She's three and a half; I'm a good bit older than that, but we can almost always bridge that gap with ease. Usually we begin with the weather.

"Is it cold up there this morning?" I ask.

"Yes," she tells me. "I have on my sweater today."

(I feel envious. In this mid-eighties Alabama humidity, we are not wearing sweaters today.)

Then we talk about her tailless cat, Charlotte, who likes to hide under the bedcovers or in the closet. Next she tells

195

me about the man next door who has a pony named Shine. And finally she asks for a report on our two spotted mutts, Max and Bentley.

I pause. I can feel the conversation winding down although I am perfectly content to continue.

Suddenly Caroline bursts forth on a totally new tangent. "Cece," she says, "the bad men nailed Jesus up on the cross. And then he died and they put him in the grave. And then Mary went to look for him at the grave but when she got there he was gone. So she saw this guy and she thought he was the gardener and she said, 'Where did you put him?' And he said her name — 'Mary.' And she turned around and looked and she saw it wasn't the gardener. It was Jesus. And he was alive again!"

There it all was! In a nutshell! In a handful of one- and two-syllable words Caroline had summed up the mysteries of the universe. What an awesome God we serve — a God who has put together a plan capable of awing toddlers and amazing adults who will come with childlike hearts. What a far-flung yet close-knit family we are, a family of struggling saints and forgiven sinners who all find level ground at the foot of the cross.

If you are willing to see yourself as part of the great patchwork quilt of the body of Christ, you will recognize yourself in Caroline's gospel story. You'll be there with Mary at the empty tomb, acknowledging the amazing truth that our Savior is resurrected. He has risen! He's alive!

O Lord God, thank you for your wonderful plan: huge enough to incorporate all creation, intricate enough to take every cell of our beings into account, vast enough to explain suns and moons and solar systems, yet personal enough to call us forth by name as your own children. Never let us cease to be amazed. Amen.

59

Prayer Works!

Praise be to God,
who has not rejected my prayer
or withheld his love from me!

Psalm 66:20

Various people in my Christian life have taught me invaluable lessons on prayer. Virginia was one such person. I remember the bleak winter she came so powerfully into my life. She was actually my sister's friend, a nurse who was in Mobile to take a course at the University of South Alabama near our home.

Every day we would meet for coffee. We would pray, read the Bible, and talk. I was trying so hard to learn to follow the Lord, but I have to admit, there was more stumbling than walking going on.

"I guess I don't really have faith that God can do what he says he can do. Or that he *will* do what he says he will," I would say. "I believe it in an abstract sense, but not in an actual sense."

Virginia never lost patience with me.

"This is new for you," she would say. "You'll catch on. Have patience with yourself. You've got the God of the universe on your side."

Then before we said good-bye, she would give me a verse to memorize. It was like a vitamin pill to sustain me until the next time we met.

One of the first Scriptures was Philippians 4:6–7. It was life altering! It encouraged me in prayer. It gave me hope to ask God for what I needed and faith to believe he would answer. It called me to give thanks and allowed me to trust God's peace even though I didn't understand yet.

Little by little, as I stopped trying to dig up the small seedlings of faith in my life, they began to take root. They began to grow and spread out in me.

Someone has said, "When we work, we work; but when we pray, *God* works." As I prayed and petitioned God about everything that winter, giving him thanks even before his answers materialized, I began to see what a powerful God he is. As I gave him room and permission to operate in me, I began to experience more of his peace and love. His supernatural strength became the bedrock of who I was (and am).

I am aware that there are those skeptics who view answered prayers as coincidences, but to those people I have to echo what an Anglican bishop once observed: "It's amazing how many 'coincidences' occur when one begins to pray!"

Father God, I thank you for friends who lead us, stand beside us, and help us to grow in faith. Thank you for the tremendous gift of prayer. In Jesus' name, amen.

60

Prayer from a Grateful Heart

Give thanks to the LORD, call on his name; make known among the nations what he has done.

Psalm 105:1

My dad loves his life. He often says, "I've never had a bad day in my life" and he means it. He acknowledges willingly and often that God has blessed him with the most beautiful wife in the world. He can still recall the moment she walked by in the hallway outside his contracts class at LSU law school. "That was it," he declares resolutely. "From that day to this, I never looked at another girl." (Perhaps I should mention that Dad just turned ninety and Mom is only two years younger!)

Dad also has a thing about his five children, twelve grandchildren, and nine great-grandchildren. He looks at them with unabashed pride and shakes his head in amazement. "Look at that group," he'll say, "not a dog in the bunch!"

Not long ago I told Daddy that I had

read somewhere a quote by St. Augustine about how much God loves a grateful heart. Augustine said that prayers of gratitude reach God's ears more rapidly than any other kind. "If that is true," I told my dad, "then surely you will be on the front row when you get to heaven."

"Well, I don't think so," he said thoughtfully. "If there's any justice at all, God will say, 'Listen, Charlie, why don't you spend a little time in the back row of the balcony now that you're here and let some of these other fellas have a shot at the good seats? You already had a lot of heaven when you were down on earth."

Like my dad, all of us should be looking at our lives daily, finding reasons for gratitude: things like the air in our lungs; the people in our lives; the gift of prayer.

Gratitude may take a little practice if you don't come by it naturally. Here's a simple suggestion on how to begin to school yourself in the skill of thankfulness. Get a notebook and every morning in God's presence, pray like this: "Lord, show me my blessings. I want to thank you. I want to have a grateful heart." Trust me — he'll answer that one.

O Father, you are so awesome, so good. Don't let

us miss a single blessing or a single reason for praise. Open our eyes and our hearts to the goodness that you pour out on your people each day. Let our gratitude grow more and more until our praise is as natural as breathing. In Jesus' name, amen.

61

Praying for the Persecuted Church

The LORD is my rock, my fortress
and my deliverer;
my God is my rock, in whom I take refuge.
He is my shield and the horn
of my salvation, my stronghold.

Psalm 18:2

As Christians we must understand that we won't always win popularity contests. Circumstances will call on us to say controversial things and to take controversial stands.

But in many countries it is not just unpopular to be Christian, it is actually dangerous. You are probably aware that all over the world, right this minute, there are people suffering for believing in Jesus Christ. People are being imprisoned and beaten and starved simply for following the Savior. Do you ever wonder if you could stand up to that kind of treatment? I do.

While in Nashville one weekend not long ago I attended a church that was hosting a Sudanese bishop. In his sermon he related a horrific story that I remember vividly. He told of the weekend of his ordination as bishop. Three Christian young men whom he had mentored decided to risk walking the twenty-five miles to reach his ordination although it would be risky for them to be found at a Christian service in that non-Christian nation. They made it in time for the service and praised God to see their friend step into his new position of leadership.

On the way back to the village, however, anti-Christian militia of the Sudanese government overtook the three young men. The soldiers demanded that the Christians renounce the "lies" they had heard and spoken at their friend's ordination. When the young men refused, the soldiers cut out their tongues and cut off their ears.

With tears in his eyes the African bishop related this tale of horror to the well-dressed members of the Nashville congregation. I did not look around me, but I am sure that many of them were considering, as I was, what they would have done had they been called to take a stand for Christ after having seen their comrades mutilated.

When remembering the persecuted church, these are the three things I pray:

1. I thank God that I live in a free nation in

which I can pray to him without persecution.

2. I pray that Jesus will supply me with the faith and courage I need should a time of persecution come.

3. And I pray for believers throughout the world who are enduring severe persecution now.

Lord God, Great Deliverer, I thank you for the freedom to pray to you. I thank you that when I need courage you will supply it. And I pray for those who are suffering for your name's sake in other parts of the world. Come to their rescue, Lord. In Jesus' name, amen.

62

Praying over Our Goals

The LORD will fulfill his purpose for me;
your love, O LORD, endures forever —
do not abandon the works of your hands.

Psalm 138:8

Every year, after the confusion of the
Christmas holidays dies down, I look forward to spending a quiet day of prayer over
my goals for the new year. I settle down in a
comfortable spot and welcome the Lord's
presence as I open the Goals section of my
notebook.

Over the years I have found that there is
tremendous power in committing my goals
and spiritual dreams to paper in the clear-
est language possible. Some goals (such as
my commitments to Bible study and
prayer) have been in my notebook for decades because they are daily ones to which
I will remain committed until the Lord
calls me home. Some I carry forward from
year to year, revising them as I go. And
there are almost always several totally new
ones that spring up based on something

new the Lord is showing me.

My first set of goals involves my relationship with the Lord. These have got to be first because I know that will affect every other thing in my life.

My next set of goals involves my relationships with other people: my husband, my family, my church family, my friends, and people we support in prayer. I try to make these goals as specific as possible. What part do I want to play in the lives of my children and my grandchildren? How can I be a better wife?

Next I have goals relating to my work as a songwriter, an author, and a speaker. The main goal in the work category is that God be glorified. But specific goals may involve seeking God's guidance as to how many "writing appointments" I want to make per month, how many times I want to speak per month, how many books and musicals I want to work on per year.

Someone asked me to teach a Bible study this year and I really had to seek the Lord about that. It sounded so appealing . . . but the Lord showed me that one more commitment would be one too many.

Seeking the Lord is imperative. We must learn to want God's will and pray as Jesus did when he said, "Not my will but yours be done."

"This is what life-planning is all about," said Anne Ortlund in her book *Disciplines of the Beautiful Woman.* "Under that wonderful umbrella of 'if God wills' we need to see what provisions are necessary for each leg of the journey, and get them. Then we need to say 'no,' . . . daily all the rest of our lives to everything that would get us off course."[1]

Father God, thank you that you have plans to prosper us and not to harm us. Help us to follow your plans. Amen.

63

Praying the Scriptures

Heal me, O LORD, and I will be healed;
save me and I will be saved,
for you are the one I praise.

Jeremiah 17:14

One of my first Bible teachers was a charming older woman named Josephine. Josephine had been raised in Mississippi during the Depression by a single mother who took in sewing to support her small brood, so there was no money for extras.

But this wise mother did not consider extras important for her children. She knew that if she could get the Word of God deep in their spirits they would be equipped for life. That is why she paid Josephine and her siblings a nickel apiece for every portion of Scripture they memorized. Nickels were precious in those days, but her children's ability to handle God's Word was more precious.

So Josephine learned the words and phrases, and she was glad to earn the money. But she did not develop a relationship with the Lord.

Years later, after she was grown, she moved to New York City where she worked in the fashion industry. It was there that she met her handsome, blue-eyed husband, Morris Townsend. The Townsends moved among many important and accomplished people in Manhattan. Morris's career in finance propelled him from one rung of success to another, including being named national director of the United States Treasury.

But financial success is no buffer for real tragedy, as the Townsends discovered when Josephine became gravely ill. A series of surgeries removed large sections of her intestines, and she lay for weeks in intense pain. As Josephine spent her days and nights under an oxygen tent, many times she awoke to find Morris in prayer by her bedside.

But the Lord was her closest companion, and his Word was constantly on her mind. Closer than her heartbeat were the precious scriptural prayers her mother had paid her to memorize many years before. Those words were her weapons and her comfort.

"Heal me, O LORD, and I will be healed," she would pray. "Save me and I will be saved."

Josephine was indeed healed and saved, and she spent more than twenty years traveling and telling of God's miraculous work in her life. Even after Morris's death when she was in her seventies, she moved to Mobile to bless many of us by teaching us the importance of learning and praying the Scriptures. She never missed an opportunity to remind us that it was the prayers of the Bible that had saved her life!

Father God, thank you for the precious gift of your Word. Let me see it as the treasure that it is. I welcome it, and you, into my heart today. In Jesus' name, amen.

64

Raise a Ruckus

Praise the LORD.
Praise God in his sanctuary . . .
. . . with the sounding of the trumpet,
praise him with the harp and lyre,
praise him with tambourine and dancing,
praise him with the strings and flute,
praise him with the clash of cymbals. . . .
Let everything that has breath praise the
   Lord.

Psalm 150: 1, 3–6

Sometimes I am so deeply moved by the drama and the emotion of the Book of Psalms that my prayers become weeping or shouts of joy. That's how it should be! The praise in us should be no less dramatic, no less dynamic, no less powerful and all-consuming than the prayers of worship in David's heart.

When we consider the awesome deeds our God has performed on our behalf, how can we keep quiet about his goodness? When we consider his mighty works and his amazing grace, how can we keep from dancing with joy? When we feel him drawing us into a deep and personal relationship with him, how can we not be ripped at the heart by the lightning of his love?

Thunderstorm of Praise

Can't you feel the worship in you building
Like an awesome thunderstorm of praise?
Can't you feel the power of the Spirit
Touch your heart's horizons with his grace?
Billowing formations of the faithful
Jagged threads of fire across your soul
As the pounding rain begins
And your heart sings out again:
"Exalt him with an anthem loud and strong
Let everything with breath join in the song!"
Claire Cloninger

We should use every instrument at our disposal to make music, glorifying the one who has given everything to us. Trumpets and harps and lyres, tambourines and strings and flutes and the crash of cymbals should resound. And most of all, our voices should sing out our praise to him.

And yet I see people get more excited about the score of a sporting event than about worshiping their awesome Creator. I see more people get on the telephone to tell a neighbor about a sale at a local store than people making a call or even a remark that would spread the best news of all — that the God of the universe has sent his Son to die for us.

Let's wake up and bring all that we are to worship him: our prayers, our joy, our music, our cheers, our deepest expressions of thanks. He has rescued and received us! He has opened his arms and called us to himself! Now isn't that something worth singing about? Isn't it time we began to let it rip and raise a ruckus?

Oh, Father God, I want to give you all that I am. I want to sing and shout and cry out with joy. I want to let the whole world hear me as I lift your praise. Use my heart, my voice, my life to exalt you. Let nothing in my worship be half-hearted. I love you, Lord.

65

Rejoice and Be Glad!

This is the day the LORD has made;
let us rejoice and be glad in it.

Psalm 118:24

This year my brother-in-law Ed is turning sixty. He and my sister Ann are planning twelve mini-celebrations, one a month all year long. As they were planning the first one, something profound hit Ann. "Ed," she said, "think of it: in twenty years we'll be eighty years old!"

He thought about it and answered in his very matter-of-fact way, "Yeah. If we're lucky."

Grim thought, you may think. But it's really a joyful thought when we consider that God has given us a mandate to "rejoice and be glad" in each new day. Each morning presents another reason to celebrate him in prayer — to rejoice in his goodness.

The New International Version of John 10:10 quotes Jesus as saying, "I have come that they may have life, and have it to the full." The King James (KJV) translation of that verse says he came "that they might have life, and that they might have it more abundantly." *The Message* (MSG) rendering of John 10:10 says that Jesus came to give us "more and better life than [we] ever dreamed of."

To live a frail, tentative, unfulfilled life is a blatant insult to the God who calls us to rejoice. To become a frantic, hurried, half-full being is a slap in the face of our Savior who died to give us more — more joy. More reason to rejoice. More hope. More prayer. More life itself.

A joyful, abundant, and prayerful life will not happen automatically. We must choose it for ourselves. How do we go about choosing such a life? We could, perhaps, choose to celebrate one thing every day: large or small, outlandish or ordinary. It doesn't matter. The important thing is to prayerfully honor the Lord by living the fulfilling life he died to give us.

We could get an "abundance notebook" in which we daily write one way to rejoice and be glad in him. We could have one child in the family plan the menu one day of each week and help prepare his or her favorite foods. We could sing hymns or favorite songs with family or friends. We could invite a different couple or single people over to lunch after church once a month. We could take nature walks with our children or grandchildren, collecting interesting rocks, leaves, wildflowers, and the like, rejoicing in God's creation. We could study a foreign country with several families in church or in the neighborhood by checking out travel videos from the library and planning a party with costumes and food from that region. We could take an art class. We could walk with a friend for exercise every morning. We could begin a prayer group in the neighborhood, begin to use a prayer journal, or find a prayer partner who will join us in jump-starting the day with five minutes of prayer on the telephone every morning.

Do you know who "the thief" is and what he's up to? Jesus will be glad to tell you. In John 10:10 Jesus also said that the thief comes only to steal and destroy. His name is Satan and he'd love to rob us of the joy of our abundant life in Christ. But Jesus came for exactly the opposite reason.

Someday we'll look down from heaven at the lives we've chosen to lead. We'll see that everything was a choice between the enemy's distraction and destruction and the joy of a prayer-filled life in Christ. I choose joy!

Father God, this is the day that you have made. I choose to rejoice and be glad in it. I choose to embrace the small celebrations and the large. Help me not to miss the amazing life that Jesus came to give me. Amen.

66

Requesting a Blessing

Jabez cried out to the God of Israel, "Oh, that you would bless me."

1 Chronicles 4:10

Of all the things written about *The Prayer of Jabez*, the one most valuable to me is that it's okay to seek our Father's blessings.

Our next-door neighbor is Pastor John Kilpatrick of Brownsville Assembly in Pensacola, home of the Brownsville Revival. Recently John was struck by the fact that Americans have so lost the element of parental blessing that we are producing a generation of rootless children. So he determined to preach a series of sermons on the meaning of blessing.

One day, quite a while after John had completed the series, a young man came to him and thanked him for his messages. "They have changed my life," he said. "In fact after the series was over I decided that I needed to drive to Ohio to talk to my father."

"Did you talk to him?" John asked.

"Yes, but it was hard for me," the young man answered. "I got to his house late at night and rang the bell. When he finally answered and saw who it was, he said, 'What do *you* want?' "

As calmly as he could, the young man said, "Daddy, I've driven all night because I need something from you."

"I knew it!" he shouted. "I always said you'd amount to no good."

"It's not like that, Daddy," the young man said. "I don't want money. It's just that I've been studying about the power of being blessed by your father. And I realized that's something I've never had from you. So I just thought if you could think up something good to say to me — that might make a difference. You don't even have to look at me when you say it. I'll go in my old bedroom and wait until you're ready."

Finally his father agreed.

"I have no idea how long I sat there," the young man said. "I could hear my daddy pacing in the hall outside my door. Finally the doorknob turned and he came in. He was standing behind me. And then I felt drops of water on my collar. Tears. My daddy's tears!"

"Son," the man finally said, "I'm so sorry. I never said a single good thing to you. I was always so critical. But maybe it's not too late. I love you, son. And I bless you."

"Pastor," the young man said, "I walked away from my father's house a changed man. Everything's changed. I've lost weight. I'm even dating a pretty girl. I feel like there's nothing I can't do."

Our Father in heaven is always ready to pour out his parental blessing on us. Let us seek him humbly and ask him for what we need.

Father, thank you for your always available blessing. You know the hole in our hearts from blessings we may not have received as children. Touch us and heal us. In Jesus' name, amen.

67

Song of Surrender

But I trust in your unfailing love;
my heart rejoices in your salvation.

Psalm 13:5

With his bushy gray beard, B.J. looked every inch the Grand Canyon river guide. He had been taking people in and out of the canyon, creating the adventures for more than a dozen years.

On this particular day we were standing above one of the most dreaded and difficult rapids in the canyon. "People have lost their lives on Lava Falls," B.J. said, and I felt my heart rate quicken.

Quietly I told one of the female guides, "I don't think I'll do this one."

"Okay," she said. "You don't have to. You can walk around on the high ground. But the last person who tried that got bit by a snake."

So I just sighed and said, "Never mind. I'll do it."

Sitting in the inflated raft watching the other rafts go ahead of us was frightening.

One minute you could see them and the next minute they were plummeting over the rapids into oblivion.

My sister Ann is a total daredevil. She knew I was afraid, so she gave me that wild-woman look of hers that said, "Get into it. Don't miss this. It's going to be the time of your life." And so I hung on for dear life, trying to have an "Ann attitude."

As our raft moved toward the huge, roaring drop-off, my hands were clutching the ropes on the raft but my spirit was trying to let go and trust. That's when I yelled out a prayer that no one but God himself could hear over the roar of the falls. "Catch me, God! Here I come!"

Suddenly the bottom dropped out and I was screaming bloody murder. And in that moment I became amazingly free. The river was whirling our raft over waves and through currents. The wind and the water were in my face. My sunglasses and my hat were knocked off and hanging by strings. And although I was gasping, I was laughing out loud. There was a new song of surrender in me moving as swiftly as the river itself.

Later, after thinking about the experience, I realized that sometimes our trip through life is like one through Lava Falls.

One direction looks incredibly risky and the other direction offers only snakebite! So you trust and choose, and God meets you, teaching you to praise him. He puts a new song in your heart, a hymn of praise to your God (Ps. 40:3).

Father, thank you for teaching us to trust you in the challenging places. Thank you for teaching us that the heart music in our lives comes from following you each day — even when it's not comfortable. I choose today to take the risks and follow you. Amen.

68

Spigot of Mercy

I pray that from his glorious, unlimited re-sources he will give you mighty inner strength through his Holy Spirit.

Ephesians 3:16 NLT

I am gazing through the front window of our log cabin, watching my husband as he sits uncomfortably on our comfortable screen porch talking on the telephone. This is the time of day that we usually take off for lunch. The time of day he turns off his lathe and brushes the wood chips off of his faded navy T-shirt and stops turning bowls. The time of day I turn off the computer and allow the words to hang temporarily in the air as we turn up the ceiling fan and settle down to talk and laugh and share a sandwich and a cool glass of lemonade.

But not today, it seems.

Today he is squirming uneasily in his easy chair. He has not even remembered to turn up the fan. His brow is furrowed and he's barely saying a word. I have no idea what this is about. I wish I did. Then I would know what to pray. But if I trust the Spirit to lead me, he will.

Suddenly a line of prayer comes into my spirit. It's a petition for all circumstances and situations, one for all seasons and all reasons — a prayer I have prayed many times before:

"Father, I pray that you will dip your great and merciful hand into your unlimited, boundless well of resources and provide Spike with whatever he needs. I don't even know the situation, but you know it. I don't even know the condition of his heart, but you know it. I don't even know whom he is talking to, but you know. I know, Lord, that your Holy Spirit is the key that turns the lock on the door of these things. So through your Spirit, now supply my husband's needs. I trust you to do these things."

In only a matter of minutes Spike is back inside the house. Silently we construct our sandwiches and make our lemonade.

What had it been? A dire emergency? No. He had merely been irritated by a grouchy old man who owns property near ours — a man who always tempts Spike to react in a flash of temper.

I don't know if Spike learned anything from the situation at all. But I learned another lesson in trusting the Lord to be in control. Instead of fretting and worrying and allowing myself to get caught up in something that was Spike's concern, not mine, I had turned my feeling of worry over to the Holy Spirit who is always able to deliver the needed amount of mercy from his abundant supply of grace. I had interceded for my husband instead of focusing on myself.

Lord, thank you that you have called us to intercede for those we love. Thank you for teaching us that your Holy Spirit is always the spigot we turn to draw on your mercy. How good you are! Amen.

69

Teach Us to Pray

One day Jesus was praying in a certain place. When he finished, one of his disciples said to him, "LORD, teach us to pray, just as John taught his disciples."

Luke 11:1

Did you ever picture yourself walking through the Galilean countryside with Jesus and his disciples, hanging on every word he taught? Amazed at his miraculous healing? Touched by his powerful love? And among all of those things that impressed you the most about the Master, did you ever imagine that his prayer life would be close to the top of the list?

I believe that as we observe the Lord's habitual dependence on his Father as revealed in Scripture, his daily reliance on prayer, we will find a growing hunger in ourselves for a deeper relationship with God in our own spirits. Just as Jesus stole away into the quiet hours of the morning to be alone with his Father, something in our hearts will be incredibly moved to do the same.

Though we may have had some sort of prayer life up to this time, just being with Jesus will cause us to hunger for something more. We will recognize in him something deeper and fuller and richer and truer, and it will ignite in us a desire for that kind of prayer. And we will not be able to resist.

"Show us, Master," we will find ourselves saying. "Show us what you know that we don't know. Lead us to the still waters that we have not yet found. Teach us, Lord, to pray. We long to pray as you do."

Then as we seek his instruction, he will meet us and lead us and teach us what we need. He wants to teach us even more than we want to learn. He "is exalted in his power. / Who is a teacher like him?" (Job 36:22) He knows that as he teaches us to pray, he is creating that connecting link between our hearts and the heart of his Father. And that is why he came.

So we ask him to hallow whatever ground we're standing on in order that we may make contact with him. And if the desire in us to pray is not strong enough, we ask him to strengthen it, knowing that he will, for he is the provider of everything we need to meet him and love him and worship him aright. There is no reason to stay at a distance when he is longing to walk

and talk with us today. Let us draw close
and bring him our hearts.

*O Lord, teach us to pray. We long to move closer
to you, to live in an intimate relationship with
you. Teach us how to love you more, how to pray
more honestly, how to give ourselves more completely to you. Amen.*

70

The Prayer for the Lord's Adventure

I know, O LORD, that a man's life is not his own;
it is not for man to direct his steps.
Correct me, LORD, but only with justice —
not in your anger, lest you reduce me to nothing.

Jeremiah 10:23–24

One of my favorite poems (by that well-known poet, Anonymous) pictures life as a bike ride. Only it is a tandem bike and Jesus is on the back, helping us pedal. Then at some point Jesus makes the suggestion that we change places with him, and once we do, life is never quite the same! We find ourselves going at breakneck speeds through rocky passes, desperate to hold on.

But Jesus only smiles and says, "Pedal."

Though he never tells us exactly where we're going, we begin to trust him. We simply leave our boring existence behind. And when we're afraid, he leans back and touches our hands.

Before long we find ourselves in the thick of the amazing adventure called life with our delightful companion, Jesus Christ. The white-knuckle ride in which we had grasped the handlebars in a death grip gradually begins to change. Our hands loosen and we know that Jesus is in control.

This is more than fiction. Jesus really does long for us to pray a prayer of surrender. He wants to get his hands on the handlebars of our lives, to chart each course and direct each path. And until we let him, we will not know the complete joy of the adventure.

I found this out in my own life. Before I had a real, surrendered relationship with Jesus, my life was going in all directions. I was on a quest for the "true fulfillment" I read about in women's magazines: the job, the career, the all-consuming interest that would make me truly happy.

Trying desperately to chart my own course and choose my own destiny, I kept steering my life onto the wrong road or into a ditch. I wanted Jesus on the bike with me, but I wanted to be the one in control. I finally found out that it doesn't work that way. In my selfish, restless quest for my own fulfillment, I began to take

Spike for granted, and we began to drift apart.

That was when I knew it was time to do what God was calling me to do: to give up my own agenda and let him take over. It was time to surrender my death grip on the handlebars of my life.

During that time I often prayed that God would fulfill in me the promise of Philippians 2:13, a promise that he will help us let go and want his will. ("For it is God who works in you to will and to act according to his good purpose.") This was a prayer he answered.

Deciding to dive into the adventure of God's will is what surrendering is all about. There is a childlike abandon obvious in us when we manage to let go. Soaked completely in his Spirit, we find our lives finally following his plans and his purposes.

Oh, Lord, I'm asking you to take the handlebars of my life today. Correct me in justice, but not in anger, I pray, O Lord. Take control of me. My life is not my own. Amen.

71

The Prayer for the Blameless Path

*I will try to walk a blameless path, but how
I need your help, especially in my own
home, where I long to act as I should.*
Psalm 101:2 (author's paraphrase)

Recently I saw a talk-show host interview
Celine Dion, the world-famous vocalist who
(in my opinion) possesses one of the most
incredible voices God ever bestowed on any
human. She is also the new mother of a tod-
dler, a little son who is the joy of her heart.
When the host asked her what it was like to
sing at the bedside of her son after singing
before thousands of people, she laughed.

"You know," she confessed, "I always
wondered what it would be like to sing to
my own child, and when I opened my
mouth for that very first lullabye, he
bawled! He really did. I sang, 'Lullabye
and good night' and he responded,
'Waaaaah!' "

This interview made me laugh. But it
also came to me as something of a personal affront. It reminded me of how

poorly my spiritual "performance" at home compares to my spiritual "performance" out in public.

When I speak to Christian groups in other cities, some of the people I address tell me what my words have meant to them. Some even write and say that God has used me to change their lives. Then I come home and often my behavior on the home front is a total flop. In fact I sometimes wonder what those audiences would think of me if they could see my messy dresser drawers or my dirty car. How inspired would they be to hear my short-tempered responses or see my self-centered choices?

The psalmist acknowledged in Psalm 101 his yearning to "lead a blameless life." But he also acknowledged to God in prayer how difficult this is to do, especially at home.

Why is this? At home our guard comes down. Our masks come off. The real "us" comes oozing through the cracks in our carefully constructed cover-up. Out there in the world we can keep up the charade, but only as long as we're not expected to do it indefinitely. At home our families come face-to-face with who we really are.

Perhaps Psalm 101:2 is a prayer you

need to pray. I know I do. On my knees before my Father in heaven I ask that I may have only one dimension to my personality — only one me. That whether I am at home with my family or with a group of women to whom I am ministering, I may walk a blameless path.

Oh, Father, help me to access your grace in order to become the best that I can be in my own home. Thank you for the family you have given me. Thank you for the times that they have loved me in spite of myself. Give me your grace to love them, too. May this home be one of mercy. Amen.

72

The Bottom Holds

Save us and help us with your right hand,
that those you love may be delivered.

Psalm 108:6

The year 2001 shook America to the core. The terrorist attack on the World Trade Center robbed us of our sense of security as we stayed glued to our television sets, mesmerized by scenes of devastation.

I remember being brought to tears one night as I watched a news special about some of the men and women who were working day and night in the rain, covered with dirt and mud, breathing in clouds of smoke, below the surface of the city. Wearing sheer fatigue like a garment, they labored on, stopping to rest only when they could go on no longer. At the ends of these grueling days they would climb out of the pit for a few hours of sleep and return before daylight the next morning.

Psalm 40:2 came to me as I watched that special: "He lifted me out of the slimy pit, / out of the mud and mire; / He set my feet on a rock / and gave me a firm place to stand."

So many prayers were going up from the families, friends, neighbors, and fellow countrymen of these workers. People who had rarely prayed seriously in the past became fervent petitioners. I believe without a doubt that the Lord was in that pit answering those prayers, giving those workers the energy to keep going as they worked blindly, tirelessly, in memory of the ones who had lost their lives.

Day after day, crowds of people lined the streets cheering their efforts as they arrived for work. It was like that for months. This applause said to them, "Your country is with you and your God is with you."

That particular news special reminded me of a true story our pastor, John Barr, related years ago. He told us about one of his theology professors whose son had been killed. The week after the funeral no one expected the professor to show up for his class, but he did.

John said that he walked slowly to the front of the class and looked out over the seminarians gathered there. The words he spoke were simple but moving. "I have been to the bottom," he said, "and it holds."

This is a message that we need now as individuals and as a nation. God has not abandoned our country and he will not abandon his people. Even at the bottom, he is there. He sees our grief and he hears our prayers. He will lift us out of the pit of our trouble and set our feet on the rock of Jesus Christ.

Father God, thank you that when our lives are at the bottom, we discover your love is already there to meet us. Send your Spirit across this land, Lord, and bring revival. Amen.

73

The Girl and the Angel

May it be to me as you have said.
                              Luke 1:38

I love the story of Mary and the angel! I wish
I could have been in the room with them the
day they looked into each other's eyes. I can
picture the Galilean sunlight streaming
through the windows as this huge, resplen-
dent, otherworldly being gazed into the innocent face of a young girl.

His wings had spanned eternal spaces.
Her feet had touched only the dust of
earth. His voice had joined the throngs of
heaven's praises. She had praised God only
in her parents' home.

Perhaps the angel wondered why the
Lord had chosen Mary. Why did he dis-
patch a message so awesome to a girl so
young — a message that would have
caused wise men to wonder and strong
men to cower? Why did he choose Mary's
womb as a cradle for his holiness and her
helplessness as a refuge for his strength?

In his great angelic mind, did Gabriel

ponder these things? Do angels ponder? Or perhaps he saw a trace of fear in her face. Whatever the reason, he spoke these words: "Do not be afraid, Mary, you have found favor with God" (Luke 1:30).

The root word for "favor" is the same as the one for "favorite." So he was saying, "Don't worry, Mary. You are a favorite of God's!"

Who was this favored one? A girl from a small town who had probably never envisioned herself living beyond the provincial formula for happiness: marriage and children. In fact, she was little more than a child herself. Perhaps that was why God had chosen her for this holy mission. Her heart was innocent. She had not outgrown her capacity to believe and trust. Her vision of an angel did not fly in the face of her childlike faith.

And although Mary had probably never imagined what she saw before her, she believed the angel's words. Unlike her cousin Elizabeth's husband, Zechariah, a temple priest, she was not struck dumb by Gabriel's message. She was in awe to be sure, but open to his words.

Now, what about you? Have you always had in your mind how life would be: same town, same friends, same church? What if you heard the Lord speaking to you, not through an angel, but through his Word, the words of a friend, or the words of this book, saying, "Will you be my person in this situation? Will you come to me in prayer and hear me? Will you step out of your comfort zone and let me use you?" Would your answer be like Mary's?

Oh, Lord, I don't want to miss what you have for me. Open my spiritual eyes and ears to see and hear you. And give me the courage to say, "May it be to me as you have said." Amen.

74

The Inner and the Outer Story

Surely you desire truth in the inner parts.
Psalm 51:6

The life of every person is like a story being told on two levels, the outer and the inner. The outer level is a story cried out in a loud voice to passersby on the street — a tale of activities and achievements. This is what people see when they look at our lives.

The inner layer is a story whispered in the dark to an audience of one in the language of prayer, a story beheld by loving eyes when we are willing to come vulnerably and open our hearts. And although God already knows its content well, he will never force us to reveal it.

The world judges our lives based on the outer story: our accomplishments. But God is much more concerned with the inner story: the attitudes of the heart (see 1 Sam. 16:7). Day by day he is reading the contents and chapters of our inner story, for that is where his interest lies.

What is God seeking on the inner level?

He is seeking the truth. If we will bring to him the truth of who we are (good, bad, and in between), he can take our honesty and create from it a life of passion, compassion, purity, and joy.

Where are you today? Are you striving to create a good-looking outer-level story that you can peddle on the street corners of your life? Are you trying to impress others with your achievements and your busyness?

Stop. Be still. God is trying to get your attention. He is waiting for you to come to him in prayer, calling you to put down all your best efforts and face the truth before him. You are a sinner — no matter how many points you may have chalked up in your outer-level story. As Paul said, "All have sinned and fallen short of God's glory" (Rom. 3:23, author's paraphrase). You are one of the "all."

Those are the simple facts of your inner story and mine. And until we are willing to throw open the windows of our wounds to the healing light of God's grace, we will never have the inner story he desires.

Meet him now in the silent inner room of the heart and call on him in prayer. Let him create in you a clean heart and renew in you a steadfast spirit (see Ps. 51).

Oh, Father, I surrender my pretenses. Forgive me for trying to look good when apart from you, I'm not. Forgive me for trying to chalk up spiritual brownie points in order to impress others or make myself feel worthwhile. I ask you to take my life exactly as it is and use it. Breathe on me, Holy Spirit. Take me and make me whatever you will. Amen.

75

No Other Gods

I will bow down . . . and will praise your
  name
for your love and your faithfulness,
for you have exalted above all things
your name and your word.

Psalm 138:2

The first of God's Ten Commandments requires that we bow down to him and to no
other gods (Exod. 20:3). It requires that we
surrender our lives to him, bend our wills to
him, and allow the life force of his love to
soak into every part of our personalities until
we are fully and freely his.

To live this way is to walk a difficult
road. It is a way of life that requires practice. But it is a journey that brings with it
the joy and fulfillment for which we were
created.

In her book *Creative Silence*, Jeanie Miley
made the following confession regarding
the worship of "other gods" in her own life:

Repeatedly, I surrender my will — my

stubborn, stiff-backed will that thinks it knows best and insists on having its own way. I give God my mind and emotions, my body, my gifts, and my efforts. I give Him my time, my problems, and my joys, because I have learned that His lordship is the only one that works. I have tried giving myself to other gods — the gods of education and knowledge, success and money, accomplishment and work. I have given good works First Place in my affection. I have tried to get other people to be God for me. I have even let the church assume top priority in my time and energy. I have placed my neck in other worldly nooses and yokes, but only the yoke of Christ grants me freedom.[1]

At times my journey on the road of surrender may be three steps forward, two steps back. But the farther I go, the more I realize that there will be no real retreat for me. I must move forward with him because ultimately there will be no other person, purpose, occupation, or material benefit that can compete with my need for God.

It's almost as though the road behind me washes out the farther I travel on it toward him. And the road ahead of me grows more solid and easier to traverse the closer I get to him. And the better I know him, the easier it becomes to surrender my life, my love, my all.

In my office are shelves lined with journals from all the years of my Christian journey. All I have to do to refresh my memory of God's faithfulness is to pull out one of them at random. Catalogued on their pages are prayers I've lifted up to the Lord over the years. And there in black and white are the stories of answers to those prayers: marriages saved, children healed, salvation brought into homes that were once Godless; all stories that prove his mercy, his love, and his Holy Spirit's power. How grateful I am for the day I called him "Lord." What an awesome God he is!

Gracious God, thank you for calling me to belong to you completely, to let go of any and all other gods, and to walk the way of surrender that leads me nearer to you. I say yes to you today. I bow down to you, awesome Father, and exalt your name and your Word. In Jesus' name, amen.

76

The Lord of Radiant Life

Praise be to the God and Father of our Lord Jesus Christ! In his great mercy he has given us new birth into a living hope through the resurrection of Jesus Christ from the dead, and into an inheritance that can never perish, spoil or fade.

1 Peter 1:3–4

People groups throughout the world worship different kinds of "gods." An assortment of handmade deities graces altars from Greece to Africa to Central and South America. Oddly, the people who worship these gods are usually aware of the fact that human hands have fashioned these statues. They may even have made the gods themselves. Still they attribute superhuman qualities of character and personality to the lifeless idols and worship them anyway.

Unlike people of other religions, we worship a living God. This passage from 1 Peter is teeming with life. It is an expression of praise to the Father of Life for his Son's merciful gift of "new birth" through his resurrection from the dead. It is a joyful celebration of our lasting inheritance in him.

Our inheritance flows to us from a Savior who was born into the human family as a baby. He was human and yet divine. He was flesh and blood as we are. He lived on this earth as we do, he died as we will, and he was resurrected to new life in a never-ending kingdom that will someday be ours.

To look at our Lord as he was on earth is to see a radiant life that vibrantly affected other people. In his book *The Gentle Revolutionaries*,[1] Brennan Manning described Jesus in these words:

> The Lord passed through the world, a figure of light and truth, sometimes tender, sometimes violent, always just, loving, effective, but not insecure. A word, a gesture, a few syllables traced in sand, a command like "Come, follow me!" and destinies were changed, spirits reborn, hearts filled with joy. Jesus walked on the water almost inadvertently; he chatted with Samaritans, prostitutes, children. He spoke to them of truth and mercy and forgiveness with never a shadow of insecurity darkening

his countenance.

The new birth Jesus gives us when we are born again is more than the hope of heaven. It is a *living* hope that touches every part of our lives here and now. We are able to see new possibilities in everyday circumstances that we never noticed before. As we enter the doorway of prayer into this new life, we become aware of the richness of its rampant possibilities. What we once viewed as dead-end situations begin to open up and a way becomes apparent. As we pray, the Lord brings light and life right through the center of our dark impossibilities. Relationships are mended. Hope is restored. When we are born again into Jesus' kingdom, we begin to live in the truth of his words as recorded in Matthew 19:26: "With God all things are possible."

Powerful God, thank you for the gift of life! Thank you for calling us out of the dimness of the half-life and into the radiant sunlight of your hope and joy. Thank you for the resurrection life you pour out in us, and for our inheritance in you that can never spoil or fade. We receive all that you have for us and determine to live this life to the fullest. Amen.

77

Meditations of My Heart

*May the words of my mouth
and the meditation of my heart
be pleasing in your sight,
O LORD, my Rock and my Redeemer.*

                                    Psalm 19:14

What I speak reveals volumes about me. My words are out there in the airwaves for everyone to hear. But the meditations of my heart — my thoughts and my feelings — are something else. They are the silent ruminations of my spirit. They are unspoken prayers that only God can hear.

French author Victor Hugo put it this way: "Certain thoughts are prayers. There are moments when whatever the attitude of the body, the soul is on its knees." When the silent soul is on its knees, these prayers are called *meditation.*

There are certain things we can do to move our spirits into a place of meditation. I remember reading a magazine article several years ago called "The Jogging Nun." It detailed the life of a nun who used her time of exercise to set her spirit on God. Each step of her jogging shoes became a prayer.

I have done that at times. One summer I began running a loop until I had reached three miles every morning. Each loop became a silent prayer for a different person on my prayer list.

My twin brothers, Charlie and Johnny, spent a week in Greece this winter walking all over an island that is almost totally dedicated to prayer and meditation. They were amazed at the lives of the priests and monks living in the beautiful old monasteries there. Most of them were totally silent, totally focused on God.

Charlie brought me a bracelet used by one group of monks to bring the meditations of their hearts into line with God. Knots were tied, one at a time, creating the bracelet, and at each knot the monk would say the Jesus Prayer: "Lord, Jesus Christ, have mercy on me, a sinner." Moving to the next knot, he would repeat the prayer. We can use every repetitive part of our work, whatever it is, to focus our hearts on Jesus. Housework, for instance, can be deadly dull, but moving through each step with a prayer in our hearts and the Lord in our lives draws us closer to him.

There are many techniques that can help to tame a noisy, unruly spirit. Any time we center our minds on the Lord and his goodness, he will touch us and bring forth in us the quiet inner prayers that give him glory.

Father God, I choose to give you not only my audible words but my silent thoughts. I invite you to reign in my spirit. Take over there and bring peace and order to my inner being until my life becomes a silent prayer. In Jesus' name, amen.

78

The Mourning Prayer

I cried like a swift or thrush,
I moaned like a mourning dove.
My eyes grew weak
as I looked to the heavens.
I am troubled; O LORD, come to my aid!

Isaiah 38:14

Have you ever heard the wailing cry of a mourning dove? It is like the sound of a widow at the funeral of her husband. It is like the moaning of the wind through the pine trees or the distant whistle of a train.

Have you ever felt that same sense of mourning in your own heart? I have. At times it has been for some very specific reason, like sharing the pain of a friend or lamenting the choices one of my children was making. Sometimes it has been over something less tangible, a vague sense of abandonment or of being misunderstood.

Regardless of my reasons, it helps me to look at the life of my Lord and realize that he, too, had feelings of deep sorrow. The prophet Isaiah painted a vivid prophetic portrait of the "suffering servant" when he described Jesus this way: "He was despised and rejected by men, / a man of sorrows, and familiar with suffering. / Like one from whom men hide their faces / he was despised, and we esteemed him not" (Isa. 53:3).

It's not hard to imagine Jesus praying a "mourning prayer" as he wept with his close friends, Mary and Martha, over the death of their brother, Lazarus. Even though he knew that he was about to perform a resurrection miracle for the dead man, his heart was broken over the sorrow of his friends and he grieved (see John 11).

But I can most clearly see my Lord's sense of abandonment and sorrow when he was on the cross. The people who had followed him around with their questions and hung on his every word of teaching were now part of an angry crowd. The friends he had known and loved and shared his life with had denied him. But most painful of all was the feeling that his Father in heaven, with whom he had been one, had deserted him.

Can you hear his mournful cry to heaven from Matthew 27:46, "My God, my God, why have you forsaken me?" Can you relate in some small way to his raw sense of pain?

How blessed we are to have a Savior who understands us. I treasure these words from Hebrews 4:15–16: "For we do not have a high priest who is unable to sympathize with our weaknesses. . . . Let us then approach the throne of grace with confidence, so that we may receive mercy and find grace to help us in our time of need."

When our hearts are broken and mournful, we can go to him. He has walked this way before.

Lord Jesus, we worship you as the almighty God and as the Man of Sorrows who was acquainted with grief. Thank you for the mercy you hold out to us in our pain. Amen.

79

The Blessing of Discipline

Blessed is the man you discipline, O LORD,
the man you teach from your law;
you grant him relief from days of trouble.
Psalm 94:12–13

Our grandson Drew really wants to know where the boundaries for his behavior lie. Just how far can he venture, and what will the consequences be if he exceeds his limits?

As loving parents, Jenni and Andy have made the boundaries very clear to both Drew and Kaylee, his sister. There is a list of "no-no's" posted on the refrigerator door that they clearly explain and frequently discuss. The children know that their parents have drawn these limits for their own good. And when they purposely overstep them, they know they may face the administration of "the spanking spoon."

Recently when Drew was staying at our house I could tell he was contemplating a little misbehavior. "Cece," he asked me very seriously, "do gwandmudders have 'panking 'poons?"

In Beth Moore's group study, *Breaking Free*, she discusses God as the ultimate loving Parent who has set boundaries for us, his children. He is the good Father who desires that we consider the consequences of ignoring the limits he has lovingly drawn. He wants us to walk in step with him so that we will not stumble and be hurt. Through this book I learned to value God's discipline.

I remember as a parent how much I hated to discipline my own children. I hated being cast in the role of the Bad Guy. I always wanted to be the Hero. But now I see that life would have been a lot easier on my children later in life if I had been a little harder on them early on.

Children need — and even like — limits. Rules cause their lives to make sense. This is also true in our lives — in our relationship with God.

That's why I often begin my prayer time by thanking God for carving out a way in the wilderness of sin, and I ask him to help me stay within the margins of his mercy. I sometimes center on the words of Jesus in Matthew 7:13–14: "Enter through the narrow gate. For wide is the gate and broad is the road that leads to destruction, and many enter through it. But small is the gate and narrow the road that leads to life, and only a few find it."

Occasionally if we wander from God's ways we will experience pain. But God's purpose is always to draw us back into the arms of his compassion, and he always uses our failures to let us know our need for him. He reminds us that his limits promise our protection.

Dear Father, thank you for your discipline. We see it as a sign of love. Thank you for giving us the awareness we need not to transgress your boundaries. Keep us always in the narrow way as we follow you. Amen.

80

The Abba Prayer

"Abba, Father," he said, "everything is possible for you. Take this cup from me. Yet not what I will, but what you will."

Mark 14:36

Two years ago in Israel we climbed the Mount of Olives. I was surprised to see what a small "mountain" it really is, yet I found myself on a spiritual high. Here was the place Jesus had spent his last night of freedom before his crucifixion.

Here he had told the twelve, "You will all fall away" (Matt. 26:31).

Here Peter had said, "Lord, no matter what the others do, I'll never desert you" (Matt. 26:33, author's paraphrase).

And here Jesus had sadly informed Peter, "This very night, before the rooster crows twice, you will deny me three times" (Mark 14:30 NLT).

Then he took Peter, James, and John with him to Gethsemane. "Don't leave me," he told them. "Stay here and keep watch" (Mark 14:34, author's paraphrase).

Not far from there, Jesus fell to the ground and prayed, "*Abba,* Father, everything is possible for you. Take this cup from me. Yet not what I will, but what you will."

This simple prayer is rich with spiritual guidance. What does it reveal about our Lord's relationship with his Father that can guide us as God's children?

First, Jesus referred to God with the intimate name of "Abba," the Aramaic term for "Daddy." In this one word we catch a glimpse of the tenderness between Father and Son. Later in Galatians 4:6 we learn that the same tender Father/child relationship is available to us for we, like Jesus, are invited to refer to God as our own "Abba."

Second, Jesus at this most vulnerable moment was acknowledging God as all-powerful. And he, more than anyone, knew how true this was. If Jesus, God's own Son, was aware of God's supreme power, how much more should we keep it in mind in our prayers?

The third thing we see in this short prayer is the Son's willingness to ask the Father for help. He didn't start out with a stiff upper lip, saying, "Bring on the cross and the nails. Whatever kind of pain and agony you've got for me is just fine and dandy." Could we ever have identified with him if he had said such things?

Instead Jesus said, "Take this cup from me." He revealed the anguish of that moment and then placed his fate, his future, and the future of the world itself into his Father's loving hands. "Your will, not mine," he prayed.

Knowing God's love for us makes this the wisest and safest prayer we will ever pray as we come to our loving Abba, God.

Dear Abba, thank you for letting us look into the mystery of this beautiful relationship you have with your Son. Thank you for inviting us to know you as your beloved children and to claim you as our beloved Papa. Thank you for our Savior who led the way. In his name we pray, amen.

81

That They May Know You

Now this is eternal life: that they may know you, the only true God, and Jesus Christ, whom you have sent.

John 17:3

In this prayer Jesus was speaking to his Father about how we, God's children, could find eternal life. His definition of eternal life was simply knowing the Father and the Son.

How often God had tried to draw people to a knowledge of himself and yet they had missed his message. "Come and know me," he had said. "Come home. I am waiting. Come and know me as I know you." How many times had he professed his love? And yet they had failed to hear.

Finally he made a heart-wrenching decision. He decided to send his one and only Son to earth to demonstrate the love we had refused to see. He decided to dress the deepest yearning of his heart in the fragile flesh of humanity and do the job in person.

He sent a child into the womb of a woman, into the family of a carpenter, into the nation of a rebellious and a prideful people who would turn their backs on him. He knew full well what a risk he was taking. He knew that before it was over they would hate and capture and torture and spit upon him. He knew that ultimately they would nail him to a cross.

So why would he have let it happen? Why would he have allowed his perfect Son to come into a world where his death was (to God at least) a certainty? Why would he have set his heart on that irrational, recklessly passionate path known as Calvary?

Think about it. What other way could we see so clearly the value that God placed on us? He so desperately desired that we walk with him in a love relationship that he paid the ultimate price.

When we catch sight of the amazing sacrificial love that Christ demonstrated on the cross for us, our lives are forever changed. Charles Wesley wrote of this life-changing revelation in his own life in his famous hymn, "And Can It Be?"

And can it be that I should gain
An interest in the Savior's blood?
Died He for me, who caused His pain?
For me, who Him to death pursued?

Amazing love! how can it be
That thou my Lord shouldst die for me?
Amazing love! how can it be
That thou my Lord shouldst die for me?

(From the *Hymnal for Worship and Celebration*, Waco, Texas: Word Music, p. 203.)

Jesus did not just happen along on this planet by chance. He came for a reason. I am the reason, and so are you. He arrived to knock at the door of our hearts and take his place in our lives. He came that we might know him and his Father and the eternal life that can be ours no other way.

Oh, Father, I praise you that eternal life is as simple as knowing you and your Son. I choose to know you and to know Jesus, and I pray for each person reading this book that his or her heart may be captured by your love and won by your mercy. Stir each person so that he or she may stop reading right this minute and say, "Yes, Lord, I want to know you. Come into my heart." Amen.

82

Releasing Our Times

My times are in your hands.
Psalm 31:15

This year I am having one of those birthdays. You know, the kind with a really high number attached to it. The kind when people blow up black balloons and come bearing cards that are supposed to be funny but are really basically unkind.

Suddenly I'm seeing my whole life in the rearview mirror and I'm overwhelmed with a desire to do the whole thing over. But as we all know, that is not an option. In fact I'm realizing how few choices we really do have in life.

We do not get to choose our looks, our brains, our families of origin. We have very little control over the length of our lives. My sister Alix is already gone — "swallowed up in victory," as Paul put it (1 Cor. 15:54). She is already singing hymns I've only guessed at, blinded by radiance I can only imagine. She has already laid her crowns at the feet of her King. And I know she's in a far, far better place than I am today.

But if it had been my choice to make, I'd have said, "Let her stay a little longer, Lord. She so much wanted to see her grandchildren growing up." From a human perspective, I would have said, "She's too young. Let her stay for our sakes."

And yet I know one thing about Alix. She lived the exact number of years, months, days, and hours that God had planned for her to live. Her times were in his hands. She knew him. She trusted him. And at the end, when the cancer had become an enemy raging through her body, she knew that her God was winning the ultimate battle regardless of what the doctors were reporting.

There was a peace underneath it all, because at the end she released her fierce grasp on the life she loved and was able to pray as David did, "My times are in your hands."

Whatever we are grasping today in our lives we must ultimately release, so we might as well begin to face that now. Whatever control we thought we had we must eventually let go like a bouquet of balloons that will float up to the heart of heaven. Not black balloons, but wildly colored ones — all the colors of this beautiful life that we've been blessed to enjoy for a season. For we are his and he is ours and in the end, our times, like our lives, are in his hands.

Father, thank you that you know the limits of our lives. Help me to agree with you. Help me to begin now to let go, releasing my fierce grip on the life you've given me. Help me to celebrate each day and at the same time to live with the surrender that must eventually be in my heart at the end. Amen.

83

The Prayer of Incarnation

I have brought you glory on earth by completing the work you gave me to do. . . . I have revealed you to those whom you gave me out of the world.

John 17:4, 6

How did Jesus the Nazarene carpenter bring glory to his Father, the almighty Creator of the Universe? Can't you just picture God with golden crowns cast down all around his feet and angels lifting amazing praises, glassy seas gleaming, and rivers rushing from the center of the city of God? And yet God is distracted. His eyes are peeled for one thing. He is watching for the glory that only Jesus can bring home to him.

What other glory could God possibly want? Jesus answered this question in the words of his own prayer to the Father from John 17. God had sent Jesus to earth to unmask God's mercy to the love-hungry people of this world who so desperately needed to know him. God had sent Jesus to earth to reveal the face of Love itself.

And Jesus had completed the task.

As amazing as this may seem, this task is the same job description that the Father has given to each of us who believe in him today. We are called to uncover the mysterious love of the Father so that others can see him up close and personal. This is what our friend Marshall Craver calls becoming "love with skin on." It is the incarnational reality into which God calls each of us.

How does God's incarnational love become a part of our daily experience? I believe that each day the Father gives us certain people to love for him. We may recognize them as "the ones" simply because they come to mind. When that happens, the Spirit is prompting us to "become love" to them, to be available to them in their place of need, to allow Jesus to work through us as he allowed his Father to work through him.

In my morning prayer time God almost always has someone that he wants me to love for him that day. It's exciting — like receiving marching orders! I keep a box of notepaper with my Bible and I often write a little note of encouragement to someone he brings to mind. Or I make a phone call.

Two different years he put my friend

Laura Preisendanz's face in my mind. When I called her in California, she said, "Claire, you never forget my birthday!" The truth is, I had no idea it was her birthday either time, but God knew. He wanted to say "Happy Birthday" to his daughter and he used me to do it!

I have often experienced God's incarnational reality in my own life. While my dad was in the hospital this year, for instance, our family felt surrounded by the arms of heaven. Not only did our own friends and family members uphold us with love and prayer, but doctors, nurses, aides, physical therapists, and speech therapists brought God into our situation in very practical ways, ministering not only to Daddy but to us.

What a joy to know that the Father chooses to be part of our lives in both the happy times and the hard times, and he will send his Spirit in the lives of his saints to do the job. And what a privilege to be one of those who is called to carry his incarnate love to others. This is God's kingdom in operation.

Oh, Father, thank you that your Son was willing to complete the work you gave him to do by coming to earth. Give us the willingness to be-

273

come "love with skin on" — to love others for you. Let us put down the trimmings of life and embrace your agenda for us. In Jesus' name, amen.

84

The Prayer of Pardon

Then he fell on his knees and cried out, "Lord, do not hold this sin against them." When he had said this, he fell asleep.

Acts 7:60

One of the most difficult choices to make when we have been hurt is whether to blame or to forgive — whether to walk the wide road of bitterness or the narrow path of pardon. Choosing, as Jesus did on the cross, to forgive those who have wounded us is choosing to line up our lives with his. It is choosing to embrace our Lord's command in John 13:34 where he charged his disciples to love others "as I have loved you."

Is it really possible to live and love as Jesus did? It's hard to imagine the level of love it must have taken for him to walk out his life on earth, much less what it would take for me to try to duplicate such a life.

But Jesus is no sadist. He has not left me an impossible assignment. Rather he allows me to see in the lives of other saints the kind of love he requires. He shows me that these are real people who, once filled with his Spirit, have what they need to live lives of mercy and pardon. And if they can do it, so can I.

Stephen was one such man, "a man full of God's grace and power, [who] did great wonders and miraculous signs among the people" (Acts 6:8). For this reason the Jews of Cyrene and Alexandria "began to argue with Stephen. But they could not stand up against his wisdom or the Spirit by whom he spoke" (vv. 9–10). So they quietly charged some men to say, "We have heard Stephen blaspheming Moses and God." Then they arrested him and brought him before the Sanhedrin.

All who were sitting in the Sanhedrin stared at Stephen. As he spoke the truth about the Messiah to the Jews, they saw that his face glowed like the light of an angel, and in their fury, they rushed at him and began to stone him.

But before they did he looked up to heaven and saw Jesus standing at his Father's side. He fell to his knees and begged mercy for his persecutors.

Though Stephen's persecution was probably more dramatic than any that we will ever face, our need to forgive those who hurt us is every bit as real as his. Harboring bitterness against others is not just a spiritual problem. It can have physical ramifications such as stress and sleeplessness as well. Emotional problems such as depression can also result. We will never be truly happy or at peace until we choose to forgive. When we are trapped in chronic bitterness, Jesus alone can provide the power we need to walk the path of pardon.

Help me, Father, not to keep an account of the wrongs done to me, but to forgive as Jesus and Stephen did, praying always that those who have hurt me will come to know you in a saving relationship. Amen.

85

The Prayer of the Samaritan Leper

Jesus, Master, have pity on us!

Luke 17:13

Jesus entered the village surrounded by his disciples. Luke does not tell us what kind of village it was, nor whether the Lord was expecting anything unusual to happen there. We know only that ten lepers met him and stood a ways from him.

Judaic law required lepers to stand at a distance and cry out "Unclean!" as a warning that their disease was extremely contagious. But not one of these lepers gave the required warning. Instead they brought their needs to Jesus, pleading, "Jesus, Master, have pity on us."

Why would these men have asked for the Lord's sympathy? The disease of leprosy numbs the nerve endings so that the sufferer is not able to respond to the warnings his own body gives. In other words, a leper may burn to death because he is unable to feel the extreme heat of a fire.

Leprosy is a wasting disease. It destroys

the cells of the body, taking away append-ages. Fingers, toes, arms, legs may literally waste away.

But perhaps the most devastating conse-quence of all to lepers in biblical times was that their contagiousness meant isolation. They lived in caves, huddled together, wrapped in rags, shunned by all society but each other.

No wonder Jesus had pity on the ten lep-rous men. No wonder he answered their prayer. He looked at them in compassion and told them to go and show themselves to the priests. And in the simple act of doing that, they were healed.

But sadly, only one of them came back and gave God the credit for his healing. He threw himself at Jesus' feet. He worshiped and gave thanks. And perhaps the most unusual element of this story is that this man was not even a Jew.

Jesus asked, "Were not all ten of these men cleansed? Where are the other nine? Was no one found to return and give praise to God except this foreigner?" Then he said to the Samaritan, "Rise and go; your faith has made you well" (Luke 17:17–19).

In some way, all of us are like the lepers. We all live at times with our feelings numbed by the harsh realities of life; at times we feel the wasting effects of the enemy's warfare, and at other times we feel bitterly isolated from others.

But the Lord showed us in this story that the way to his healing is open when we pray the way the Samaritan leper did: with faith to ask the Lord for what we need. Faith to listen for his instructions and follow them. And faith to return to him with gratitude in our hearts.

Father God, thank you for hearing our prayers. Keep our hearts tender that we may hear your healing words, and may we always return to you in gratitude. Amen.

86

The Sinner's Prayer

Have mercy on me, O God,
according to your unfailing love;
according to your great compassion
blot out my transgressions.

Psalm 51:1

David's affair with Bathsheba is one of the Bible's steamiest love stories. His decision to send Bathsheba's husband, Uriah, to his ultimate death at the front lines of Israel's battle shows us just how far David went to get the woman he never should have had (see 2 Samuel 11).

David's sin, his contrition, and his yearning to be restored to the joy of God's salvation are at the heart of his prayer in Psalm 51. It contains his fervent plea for God's mercy.

It may be tempting to take the Pharisee's stance and see Psalm 51 as inapplicable in our lives. But if we are honest we will see that our sin is no different from David's in God's eyes. We will recognize the truth of Paul's statement: "All have sinned and fall short of the glory of God" (Rom. 3:23).

Only as we recognize that truth can we come to the Lord, seeking forgiveness for our own sin, and praying David's prayer, "Have mercy on me, O God, / according to your unfailing love; / according to your great compassion / blot out my transgressions." Only as we stand in that place of penitence will God's forgiveness ever set us free and bring us into right standing with our Father.

The following lyric traces the heart cry of David as expressed in Psalm 51:

Song of the Sinner

There's a desperate cry from the soul of
    every sinner,
For we can't deny the pain of our trans-
    gressions.
There's a silent wound in the depths of
    every person,
For we cannot hide the sin that drives
    our passion.

That's something only God can do,
A darkness only He can reach,
The shadows only He can touch,
To heal our deep iniquities.

That's something only God can do,

To quench our thirst for holiness,
A mission we must trust Him with,
To touch and heal our brokenness.

Come, Holy Spirit,
Come in your compassion
Blot out my transgression;
Let the bones you crushed within me
   dance again.

Come, Holy Spirit,
I will teach transgressors
To walk the way of wisdom.
Let this broken heart within me beat
   again.

Come, Holy Spirit,
In your mercy wash me,
In your power cleanse me,
Let the sun of righteousness now rise
   again.

Come, Holy Spirit,
I have sinned against you,
How I need your mercy.
May this broken, contrite spirit sing
   again.
                              Claire Cloninger

Thank you, Lord, for David's prayer. Thank

you for showing us in his life and in his prayers that in spite of his sin, you loved him, you forgave him, and you restored him to new life in you. Teach us to see ourselves honestly and come to you openly as he did, for only in you can we be restored to new life. In Jesus' name, amen.

87

The Sweetness of Your Words

When your words came, I ate them;
they were my joy and my heart's delight.
                                    Jeremiah 15:16

Recently Spike and I watched one of our favorite musicals, *Fiddler on the Roof*, on video. Topol's performance as Tevye is nothing short of amazing. He plays the entire scale of emotions on my heartstrings every time I watch him in the leading role.

Fiddler on the Roof is the story of a small Russian village. Tevye, a poor milkman, and his wife, Golde, are the parents of five girls. With no dowry for any of the five, Tevye realizes that he is facing an uphill battle to get these precious daughters married.

Throughout the musical Tevye is talking and singing to God. His prayers allow the audience to take an intimate look into the thoughts and feelings he shares with his God.

One song that combines both laughter and tears is "If I Were a Rich Man." In it,

Tevye talks to God about what it would have been like to be truly wealthy. He visualizes the huge house he would have built with a fine tin roof and wooden floors. He pictures Golde with "a proper double chin" as only a wealthy wife could afford. He sees her dressed in finery, bossing her servants around.

Then Tevye, becoming very quiet, tells God what would have mattered most to him. If he had been rich, he would have had time for prayer and discussing the holy books, time to spend with his Maker. "And that would be the sweetest thing of all," he says.

Pretend with me now. Suppose you won the lottery *today*. Suppose you didn't have to go to work or worry about money. How would that change your life? Would you spend the money on travel? On fine possessions? On a new home?

Let's face it. In America few of us are hungry. All our pockets are relatively full compared to those of many people around the world. Instead, what we really need is more time for prayer, more time for God's Word, more time to spend with our Maker.

I pray that a yearning may begin to grow in your heart and in mine for more time and a deeper relationship with the God who longs to get our attention. Only when we yearn for him, only when we seek him, only then will we find him. And that will be "the sweetest thing of all."

Father, turn us from our materialism. Slow us down. We want to spend more time with you. We want to know your Word more fully, to experience your love more deeply, to travel the roads that lead us to the heart of your heart. Draw us to you. Amen.

88

The Temple

How lovely is your dwelling place, O LORD Almighty!

Psalm 84:1

When King Solomon built the temple in Jerusalem to honor his God, it was a place of great beauty created with stone, cedar, silver, and gold. Solomon and the people of Israel consecrated it with burnt offerings, grain offerings, and fellowship offerings. It was a holy house where the people, through their priests, could meet with the Lord and hear from him — a place where they would feel the wondrous cloud of his presence (see 1 Kings 5–9).

No wonder the psalmist said of God's temple, "My soul yearns, even faints, / for the courts of the LORD; / my heart and my flesh cry out / for the living God" (Ps. 84:2). In Solomon's day there was no higher calling than to draw near to the Holy of Holies. This is still true, but many of us are confused about just exactly where the Holy of Holies is.

When Stephen defended his faith before the Sanhedrin, he told them, "The Most High does not live in houses made by men" (Acts 7:48).

When the God of all creation chose to take on our humanity and "move into the neighborhood," as Eugene Peterson put it, he was creating a new kind of temple — one not made with wood, stone, silver, and gold, but a temple of flesh and bone and spirit.

By choosing to join the human family and becoming our once-for-all sacrifice (Rom. 6:10), Jesus was rendering the temple of Solomon's day unnecessary. He was becoming the first human temple created to contain the Holy Spirit of his Father, God Almighty. And what's more, he was inviting us to do the same.

By his perfect sacrifice he tore down the walls of sin and death between us and God and he built up a holy meeting place where God could "tabernacle" within his people — no buildings, no sacrifices, no mediators required. We need only a willingness to be with him and pray to him and hear from him.

As Paul put it in 1 Corinthians 6:19, "Do you not know that your body is a temple of the Holy Spirit, who is in you, whom you have received from God? You are not your own."

The temples of our bodies in which God has chosen to dwell are works of art we could never have created on our own. We can only welcome our living God to meet us within.

Oh, Father, I echo David's desire, saying, "My soul yearns, even faints / for the courts of the LORD." I long to know you more and more. And yet I know that many times I am an unfit dwelling place for you. Come and clean the tabernacle of my spirit so that you may be at home here. Forgive my sin so that you may say of me, "How lovely is my dwelling place within this, my child." Amen.

89

The Ultimate Prayer

After this I looked and there before me was a great multitude that no one could count, from every nation, tribe, people and language, standing before the throne and in front of the Lamb.

Revelation 7:9

On days when my life seems tiring or boring, all I have to do is remember where it is headed and I find myself becoming excited. All I have to do is to remember that there is more joy and worship and unending praise in store for me than I can even imagine.

All prayer from the beginning of time to its final days will culminate in one amazing and glorious and unending scene. The cast of characters is a great multitude of people too vast to be numbered. John described them like this:

They were wearing white robes and were holding palm branches in their hands. And they cried out in a loud voice:

"Salvation belongs to our God,
who sits on the throne,
and to the Lamb."

All the angels were standing around the throne and around the elders and the four living creatures. They fell down on their faces before the throne and worshiped God, saying:

"Amen!
Praise and glory
and wisdom and thanks and honor
and power and strength be to our God
    for ever and ever. Amen!"

(Revelation 7:9–12)

These are beautiful words, powerful words. They are words worth memorizing and placing in our hearts so that any time we are tempted to feel that we've got dead-end lives, we can enter that scene of ultimate worship and prayer and praise. We can remember that we are already on our way to a spiritual high that will never end. If we belong to Jesus we will be among that great multitude singing the awesome song of unending glory!

Father God, you are the great and glorious God

in whom there is no beginning and no end. You were, you are, and you are to come. Thank you for the salvation that is ours because of what Jesus has done on our behalf. We wait with joy for the day when we will enter into your gates with thanksgiving and praise. Then we will worship you face-to-face. In Jesus' name, amen.

90

The Woman Who Waited

Then Hannah prayed and said:
"My heart rejoices in the LORD. . . .
There is no one holy like the LORD;
. . . there is no Rock like our God."

1 Samuel 2:1–2

There were no over-the-counter pregnancy tests in my day. You went to the doctor's office, took a blood test, and waited for a phone call.

We had already done a lot of waiting. We had been married for nearly six years, longing all the while for a child. Once a month, when I realized that good news was not coming, I spent the day crying. Then one happy day I realized that I did have reason to hope, and I made a doctor's appointment.

Needless to say, there was great rejoicing when the phone rang and my doctor announced, "Claire, you and Spike are going to be parents!" I threw the phone down and began to scream at the top of my lungs, jumping and shouting with joy through the house!

Hannah's story in 1 Samuel is very different from mine, but it is also the story of a woman who had longed for a child. Hannah's husband, Elkanah, had two wives. His other wife, Peninnah, had lots of children, but Hannah was childless.

Year after year Elkanah went up to worship and sacrifice to the Lord at Shiloh. Peninnah never failed to make the trip miserable for Hannah by bragging about her children.

And then one year at Shiloh, Hannah went to the temple, where she wept bitterly before the Lord, "O LORD, if you will look at my misery and give me a son, then I will give him to you for all the days of his life" (1 Sam. 1:11, author's paraphrase).

Eli, the temple priest, came in, saw Hannah's mouth moving, and made the assumption that she was drunk. When he rebuked her, Hannah replied, "Not so, my lord. . . . I was pouring out my soul to the LORD" (1 Sam. 1:15).

"Go in peace," Eli answered, "and may the God of Israel grant you what you have asked of him" (1 Sam. 1:17).

Hannah believed that the Lord had heard her prayer. And she kept her promise: when Samuel was born she presented him to the temple priests. I cannot imagine this kind of sacrifice — to literally give your son away after waiting so long for his birth. But Hannah's faith was great and her son was greatly used.

Hannah was a woman who trusted God without giving up, praised God when her prayer was answered, and returned to God the blessing he had given her that he might use it to his glory. May we do the same as we yield our lives to him and return his blessings to him to use to his glory.

Oh, Father, my heart rejoices in you. Thank you for your answers to my prayers. Help me to release my grasp on the gifts you give me and place them back in your hands. And, like Hannah, give me the patience to wait for your will. Amen.

91

Things Go Better with Praise

Yours, O LORD, is the greatness and the power
and the glory and the majesty and the splendor,
for everything in heaven and earth is yours.
Yours, O LORD, is the kingdom;
you are exalted as head over all.

1 Chronicles 29:11

Phyllis McGinley, a Pulitzer Prize–winning poet, wrote one of my favorite books on the joys of raising a family and keeping a home. Her book, *Sixpence in Her Shoe*, was in its eleventh printing when I first bought it. Though I've read through it many times, I still pick it up from time to time and find something profound in its pages. Today I read one such remark: "Praise is like love; it helps the world move smoothly."

I never would have thought to word it that way, but I believe her words are true. I've seen it play out in my own life, for somehow when I'm praising the Father, the world around me seems to turn with more grace and beauty.

Did you ever wonder: Aren't we really telling the Lord what he already knows when we praise him? Doesn't he already know how great, how awesome, how majestic he is? Of course he does! But how much more wonderful our world seems when we are in the process of telling him that we know these things, too!

When we come to our Father and give him the glory he deserves, it's like giving someone a gift that is already his. All glory belongs to the Lord. It certainly doesn't belong to us, does it? All the more reason to give it back to the one who has a right to it. And when we do, somehow we are greasing the wheels on this sometimes rough-riding vehicle known as life.

Does our prayer from 1 Chronicles 29 go just a little bit overboard? Or is it even possible to go too far for the one who has gone totally overboard for us? He created us. He loved us. He gave us everything. And when we broke his heart, he did not give up on us. He sent his Son to atone for our sins. Is there too much praise for such a God? I don't think so. And how it eases my way when I give to him the amount of praise he deserves — all I've got!

Lord God, I rejoice in your greatness. I celebrate your grace, your mercy, your righteousness, your holiness, and your love. Reveal to me every day new ways to honor you with my prayer, my praise, and my life. I love you, Lord. Amen.

92

To Be Like Him

But you, O God, do see trouble and grief;
you consider it to take it in hand.
. . . You are the helper of the fatherless.

Psalm 10:14

Amanda stood before the congregation, struggling to express her feelings about the youth group's mission trip to Costa Rica.

"I think I'll just tell you about the day we ministered to the people at the garbage dump," she began. "It was an incredible sight to see these people that the Costa Ricans refer to as 'scavengers' crawling all over the mounds of refuse, pulling out cast-off items and even old food from under stacks and stacks of garbage. I soon realized, though, that the smell of the dump was going to be much harder for me to take than the sight. The closer we got, the more unbearable it became.

"Whitney, the missionary leading our group, could see that I was about to lose it! 'Amanda,' she said, 'just inhale as deeply as you can and the smell will get bearable.'

I did it and she was right. The smell no longer offended me. I could look at the people and see them with the love of Jesus.

"We had brought them a big birthday cake and some candles (though it was no one's birthday, we rightly assumed that few if any of them had ever celebrated with a cake). We sang 'Happy Birthday' with them, blew out the candles, and cut the cake. They were so happy. We all laughed together and had the most wonderful time.

"On the way back I realized that what we did was, in a small way, like what Jesus did when he came to earth. He saw the mess we were in, and he came. We were the garbage — the smelly human junk clothed in filthy rags. But he was willing to leave heaven and enter our pathetic trash heap of life and love us. He was willing to spend his life scavenging for human souls."

The church was quiet. Amanda sat down. I was thinking of my Savior's love, not only for the Costa Rican scavengers but for me. Amanda's report reminded me again of the powerful verses Paul communicated to the Philippians:

Each of you should look not only to your own interests, but also to the interests of others.

301

Your attitude should be the same as that of Christ Jesus:

Who, being in very nature God,
did not consider equality with God
  something to be grasped,
but made himself nothing,
taking the very nature of a servant,
being made in human likeness.
And being found in appearance as a
  man,
he humbled himself
and became obedient to death —
even death on a cross! (Philippians
2:4–8)

Oh, Father, you see our trouble and grief and you don't ignore it. You enter into our problems. You truly are the Father of the fatherless. Forgive me when I allow anything to keep me from ministering to the people for whom Jesus died. Teach me the beauty of his humility and how to walk in it. Amen.

93

Trusting God in the Battle

Save us and help us with your right hand,
that those you love may be delivered.

Psalm 60:5

The Bible is chock-full of stories of every kind: romances, adventures, and family intrigues. One of the most common variety is war stories. They often teach us vivid lessons.

One such story appears in Exodus 17:8–13. In it the Amalekites had come and attacked the Israelites at Rephidim. Moses said to Joshua, "Choose some of our men and go out to fight the Amalekites. Tomorrow I will stand on top of the hill with the staff of God in my hands" (v. 9).

Here's how the battle went: As long as Moses held the staff of God high above his head, the battle belonged to the Israelites. But the minute his hands grew tired and he lowered the staff, the Amalekites began to win.

So two other leaders, Aaron and Hur,

helped solve the problem. When Moses' hands grew tired they provided a stone for him to sit on. Then Aaron and Hur held his hands up, one on each side. That way Moses' hands remained steady all day long until sunset.

Joshua won the battle against the Amalekite army on the battlefield. But Moses and Aaron and Hur were his backup troops up on the mountain.

This was a foreshadowing of how the body of Christ is to work. While one ministers, others pray for the one on the front lines. And there are even backup intercessors who can pray when the first team grows tired.

A number of years ago while visiting the Brooklyn Tabernacle, the vibrant inner-city church pastored by Jim Cymbala, we heard Jim explain how their Intercessory Prayer Room worked. The whole time the service was ongoing, "prayer warriors" were in the quiet room overhead praying for the service.

Many times the prayers of the intercessors turned the tide of the "battle" below. Once, for instance, a man on drugs burst into the service, swinging a gun and spewing curse words. The ushers were able to remove the man and no one was hurt.

God gave the church leadership the grace to handle this stressful situation in the sanctuary, just as he gave Joshua the strength to defeat the Amalekites on the battleground. But just as Moses, Aaron, and Hur made the difference from their places on the mountain, it was the intercessory prayer team above the sanctuary in the upper room who made the difference at the Brooklyn Tabernacle that day.

Father God, equip us and teach us to pray as intercessors. Strap on us the full armor of your kingdom and lead us forth into battle. We choose to follow you. Amen.

94

Two Women, One Guest

How sweet are your words to my taste,
sweeter than honey to my mouth!
. . . The unfolding of your words gives light;
it gives understanding to the simple.
Psalm 119:103, 130

Two sisters prepared for one guest. Mary
moved from task to task with a thankful and
a settled heart, quietly doing the chores that
would make him feel at home. Joyfully she
pictured his face. What would he share with
them today? Serenely she readied her heart
and her home for his visit.

Martha, with sweat on her brow and resentment in her heart, was grumbling in
the kitchen. No doubt Mary would leave
her with all the work again, she thought.
No doubt she would sit idly by, listening to
the Master. Once he had arrived, Martha
thought, she would tell him about Mary's
thoughtlessness. He would understand. He
would speak to Mary in that convincing
way of his and tell her to give Martha some
help.

When the Master arrived, they seated him on their most comfortable cushion. Mary immediately sat at his feet. From the kitchen Martha could see the Master's lips moving as he looked intently into Mary's eyes and spoke to her. And there was Mary, drinking it all in. Finally Martha could stand it no longer. She burst into the room.

"Master," she said to Jesus, "don't you see it? Don't you care? Mary is doing nothing while I'm working in the kitchen. A meal doesn't just happen, you know. And we are not a wealthy household with many servants. Tell her to help me."

"Martha, Martha," the Lord answered, smiling at her. "You have allowed yourself to become upset about so many little things. Only one thing — only our relationship — is really important. In the end, that is all that will not be taken away" (see Luke 10:38–42).

Jesus was not telling Martha that she was evil or even wrong. He was simply telling her that her choice was second-best. She could have been listening to his words and instead she was listening to the push and hurry of her life. She could have been spending precious time with him and instead she was puttering and sputtering. Is that convincing to you? It is to me.

When the Lord is knocking at the door of my heart, seeking a chance to spend time with me, and I tell him I've got to clean a closet or write a song, I should hear his voice saying, "Claire, Claire. Don't get sidetracked on the 'many things.' Only one is really important. Choose it! Sit at my feet. I've got things I want to say to you!"

Oh, Lord, I choose you and our relationship. I want to draw near to you, to sit at your feet and hear your words. They are the treasures of my heart. I love you, Lord. Amen.

95

Unceasing Prayer

Hear, O Lord, and answer me. . . .
You are my God; save your servant who
trusts in you.
Have mercy on me, O Lord,
for I call to you all day long.

Psalm 86:1–3

When we read Paul's letter to the Thessalonians challenging them to "pray continually" (1 Thess. 5:17), is he calling for the kind of prayer that creates calloused knees? When we read David's words in Psalm 86:3, "I call to you all day long," is he speaking to God in the kind of prayer that makes us hoarse? No. I believe that both passages describe a silent, intimate, ongoing dialogue with our God.

Paul knew that the Christians at Thessalonica had no hope of making it apart from their prayers and God's answers. This was why he encouraged them to learn to pray continually.

David knew that he had no chance of overcoming his enemies apart from God's intervention. That's why he needed unceasing prayer. David was also aware, no doubt, of his own susceptibility to sin. So he brought it before the Lord every chance he got.

Prayer was a constant in the lives of so many believers in the Bible. How can we make it more of a constant in ours?

The truth is, we are taking part in an inner thought-dialogue all day anyway. Though that dialogue may not be prayer and we may rarely be aware of its presence, we must acknowledge that there are words moving through our minds.

Let me give you an example. Let's say, for instance, we're trying to figure out what route we'll take to work. *Uh-oh, there's a wreck just ahead. I can turn off to the right and avoid the backup. Put the blinker on. Turn. Okay. I can probably make it without any more traffic problems. Just hope I won't be late.*

How can we direct the inner dialogue in the paragraph above to the Lord, thereby making it a prayer? Track with me. "Uh-oh, Father, a wreck. Show me what to do. Blinker on. Right turn. Thanks, Father. Be with the people who were in the wreck. I pray no one was hurt. Be with the rescue people. Thank you for their gifts of healing. Thank you, Lord, for guiding me.

Help me get to work on time. I love you, Lord. Thank you that I'm never alone."

Do you see? It's the same situation, only one way it's an opportunity for stress and the other way it's an opportunity for prayer.

Father God, I worship you. Keep me close to you today. Call my attention to you and help me recognize the many opportunities I have to pray without ceasing. I choose to lift my heart to you in every small thing. Amen.

96

Unshakable Faith

Then Jesus looked up and said, "Father, I thank you that you have heard me. I knew that you always hear me, but I said this for the benefit of the people standing here, that they may believe that you sent me."

John 11:41–42

At the tomb of Lazarus Jesus called men to remove the stone. Then he looked up and prayed, thanking God in advance for what he knew would happen. Everyone there was stunned to see a dead man emerge wrapped in grave cloths — everyone, that is, but Jesus (see John 11). Jesus knew that Lazarus would come forth alive. His faith in his Father's power to raise him was unshakable. In fact, he was so sure of God he could have prayed silently. So why did he pray aloud?

Jesus thanked his Father audibly for the benefit of the people standing there, so that they would believe in the Holy One whom God had sent.

Do you have confidence enough to pray aloud for a friend in need, knowing that only God can — and will — work a miracle for your friend? Do you have confidence enough to pray aloud in a group, asking God to work powerfully on behalf of you or someone else? Is your faith the unshakable kind that Jesus had? Nothing in the world is more faith building for others than to hear us speak out boldly, trusting God to answer.

How can we come to that place of supreme confidence in the Lord's ability to answer our prayers? Only when we operate as containers of his Holy Spirit will we find that level of trust. Only when we say with Paul, "I have been crucified with Christ and I no longer live, but Christ lives in me" (Gal. 2:20).

As Jesus lives in us, he will also pray through us. The one who calls us to pray with unshakable faith is the one who will pour out his own faith in us and speak out his own prayer through us. The one who calls us is faithful and he will do it! (1 Thess. 5:24)

Lord Jesus, I trust you to pray with power in and through me. Help me not to worry about what words I will say to you, but teach me simply to allow you to have your way in me. I trust you and I yield to your Spirit. Amen.

97

The Blessing of a Home

I long to dwell in your tent forever
and take refuge in the shelter of your wings.
Psalm 61:4

Recently we attended a "house blessing," a service to dedicate a family's home to God. We were given verses and candles to carry. As we walked from room to room inviting God's blessing, the service went like this.

(Leader knocks from outside the front door or from the foyer.)

Child: "Who knocks at our door?"

Leader: (representing Christ) "Here I am! I stand at the door and knock. If anyone hears my voice and opens the door, I will come in and eat with him, and he with me" [Rev. 3:20].

Leader: "When you enter a house, first say, 'Peace to this house' " [Luke 10:5].

All: Peace to this house.

In the Living Room:

Whoever welcomes one of these little children in my name welcomes me; and whoever welcomes me does not welcome me but the one who sent me (Mark 9:37).
All: Welcome. Lord Jesus.
Prayer for the living room: "Lord, we invite you to be Lord of this home. Enter and bring your holiness. If any darkness has entered in the past, cleanse it by your presence. Heal the hearts of all who dwell and visit here. Amen."

In the Study or Library:

"Do not conform any longer to the pattern of this world, but be transformed by the renewing of your mind" (Rom. 12:2).
Prayer for the study: "Guard our hearts and minds, Father. Keep them stayed on you. Amen."

In the Kitchen:

"Do not work for food that spoils, but for food that endures to eternal life, which the Son of Man will give you" (John 6:27).

Prayer for the kitchen: "Thank you for being the True Bread that nourishes us."

In the Bedroom:

"I will lie down and sleep in peace, / for you alone, O LORD, / make me dwell in safety" (Ps. 4:8).

Prayer for the bedroom: "Bless us as we sleep and dream in safety."

In the Guest Room:

"Share with God's people who are in need. Practice hospitality" (Rom. 12:13).

Prayer for the guest room: "We praise you for the gift of shelter. Give your rest and peace to those who share our home."

In the Child's Room:

"I tell you the truth, unless you change and become like little children, you will never enter the kingdom of heaven" (Matt. 18:3).

Prayer for the child's room: "Lord, bless the child who dwells here. May we be a good example to her [him] of your grace as we spend our days together."

In the Dining Room:

"I have food to eat that you know nothing about. . . . My food is to do the will of him who sent me to finish his work" (John 4:32, 34).

Prayer for the dining room: "Lord Jesus, focus our meals on your presence. May we dwell more on your mercy than the menu. Extend the blessings of the table to all who gather here."

Home Owner or Renter:

"Thank you, Father, for this home. We dedicate it to you. You have told us to choose whom we will serve and today we choose to serve you [Josh. 24:15]. Amen."[1]

After the house blessing that night, we enjoyed refreshments, conversation, and laughter. Was it only my imagination that there was a whole new Spirit in the place? No. The Lord and his Holy Spirit were there in force! Whenever and wherever we invite him in, he accepts our invitation, spreading the light and love of his presence to all who are there.

Lord God, we thank you for the gift of prayer.

Thank you for our homes and your willingness to dwell with us. Stir up in the hearts of all those reading these pages now a desire to invite you daily into the rooms of their homes and their hearts. In Jesus' name, amen.

98

You Are God

Before the mountains were born
or you brought forth the earth and the
world,
from everlasting to everlasting you are
God.
. . . For a thousand years in your sight
are like a day that has just gone by,
or like a watch in the night.

Psalm 90:2, 4

In recent months I have heard people ask
each other, "Where were you when the
World Trade Center was attacked?" It's as
though they believe that if they can pinpoint
that time and place in their lives, they'll re-
gain their balance.

When something awful happens — such
as a catastrophe like this one — I am
sometimes tempted to think that God is
also shaken or alarmed. I am tempted to
think that the events of the world have
taken him by surprise. I may even want to
ask him why he was napping when we
needed him so desperately to be on the job.

To believe that a tragedy shocked or shook God, or caught him off guard, is to miss his true nature. Our future may be uncertain to us, but it is never uncertain to God. Our Father knows.

God can see the coming of all things in his mind's eye long before they reach us. From everlasting to everlasting he has known and seen, for he is God. He visualizes our lives from both sides of time, forward and backward, future and past. Years and minutes are the same to him.

It's also tempting at times to think that the attitudes of my heart have shocked God, but I know for certain that they have not. My thoughts and actions may cause him grief, but they have never surprised him. God created our hearts, and is very familiar with us (Ps. 103:14). He knows how we are formed, he remembers that we are dust. He knows our hypocrisy, our faithlessness, and our failure to forgive. He knows, and yet he is always standing by, waiting to forgive.

So many things about this world are uncertain and unsure. So many things about our lives puzzle and confound us. We do not have God's vision or perspective. We cannot see beyond the boundaries of today or through the windows of tomorrow.

But this one thing is sure. God is everlasting, ever certain, never changing. We can bring our sin and our sorrow, our hopes and our helplessness, our prayers and our praises into his faithful presence, trusting in his love. He is not about to give up on us. Our great unshakable God is on our side.

Oh, Father, what an awesome comfort to know that you know all things — that you never change. You have been here from before the foundations of the earth and you will never leave us nor forsake us. I worship you, O Lord. Amen.

99

You Are Pleased with Me

I know that you are pleased with me,
for my enemy does not triumph over me.
In my integrity you uphold me
and set me in your presence forever.

Psalm 41:11–12

I'll never forget the day my friend (I'll call her Samantha) confessed to me that she was emotionally drained.

"I'm exhausted from trying to earn my parents' approval," she said. "At some level I know they must love me. But when I strip away the birthday presents and the outward expressions, I'm left with this awful feeling in the pit of my stomach that there is something more I need to do to earn a place for myself in their hearts."

I wonder how many of us walk around every day with that same uneasy feeling — that we still must justify our existence, not only to our loved ones but perhaps to ourselves and even to God.

In his book *Life of the Beloved*, Henri Nouwen observed, "Self-rejection is the greatest enemy of the spiritual life because it contradicts the sacred voice that calls us the 'Beloved.' "[1]

In Psalm 41:11–12, David prayed with confidence, knowing that his God was pleased with him. He accepted the favor of the God who was continually drawing him into his presence.

To pray in the assurance of the Father's love is to know the inner rest and peace and grace God intends for us to have. It is allowing the affirming words of God's acceptance to define and lead us rather than listening to the condemning words of the world or the enemy.

These words of Zephaniah 3:17 peel back the heart of God's compassion and reveal a deeper level of love and acceptance than we might ever have imagined: "The LORD your God is with you, / he is mighty to save. / He will take great delight in you, / he will quiet you with his love, / he will rejoice over you with singing."

In this verse I discover that God is more than "pleased" — he is "delighted" with me. He is even rejoicing over me with singing. There is nothing halfhearted in his approval!

What about you? Are you willing today to hear God expressing his affection for you? He loves you simply because you are his. He takes great delight in you. Regardless of your own disappointments, he is rejoicing over you. And he wants you to live out your life in the joyful awareness of his acceptance.

Lord, I thank you that you are pleased with me and that you love me. Thank you for David and Zephaniah's words that let me know how you feel about me. I choose to live my life in the reality of those truths. I love you, Lord. Amen.

100

You Will Still Be Here

Where can I go from your Spirit?
Where can I flee from your presence?
If I go up to the heavens, you are there;
if I make my bed in the depths, you are
there.

Psalm 139:7–8

The constancy of our Father's presence is one of the most important lessons we can learn as we practice a life of prayer. Regardless of the situation, God will always be there.

Our son Curt learned this when he was doing short-term mission work on the island of St. Croix. Curt's Youth With a Mission team was divided into two ministries, the clown ministry that did street shows for kids, and the prison ministry that preached the gospel in prison.

Halfway through the team's month on St. Croix, Curt's prison ministry had a day off, but Curt decided to minister with the clown team, using his free time to talk to the kids.

The team set up the puppet stage in a covered area near a housing project where most of the kids lived. The younger children excitedly gathered around the stage waiting for the play to begin, while older guys with dreadlocks leaned against the walls looking skeptical and laughing at the "clown teens" who had come to talk about Jesus.

Curt saw three girls, about twelve years old, sitting together. After the production he went over and introduced himself. He could tell that one of the girls, Chanelle, was very interested in Christ, so he and his friend, Craig, stayed quite a while to answer her questions.

Chanelle said she wanted to go to church, but her grandmother wouldn't allow it. "That's okay," Curt explained. "Jesus can live in your heart. And when he does, he can change things." Before getting back on the bus, Curt led Chanelle to the Lord.

Leaving the projects that day he was happy about Chanelle's conversion but worried that she would have no friend in the faith.

Nearly three weeks later, just before their scheduled departure from St. Croix, the team returned to Chanelle's project. Curt prayed he would see her, and sure enough, he did. He asked how she was doing.

Her smile was enormous. "God is very good, Curt," she said. "My grandmother lets me go to church now and she doesn't cuss anymore at all. I am studying the Bible with a small group. My life is so much better."

As Curt was riding away on the bus that day, he remembered how worried he had been about Chanelle. "Lord, you were trying to tell me, 'I'll take care of it, son. You may leave, but I will still be here.' "

Lord God, thank you that we cannot separate ourselves from you. You will always be near us and near our loved ones, caring for us and keeping us no matter what may come. Amen.

101

Who He Is to You

You are the Son of God; you are the King of Israel.

John 1:49

Worship begins when we look to Jesus and tell him who he is to us. In John 1, Nathanael recognized the divinity of Jesus merely because Jesus had seen him under a tree and called him by name. That's when he confessed him as the Messiah.

Later Jesus asked Peter, "Who do you say I am?" Peter readily replied, "You are the Christ, the Son of God" (Matt. 16:15–16).

All who had been at our Lord's baptism in the Jordan heard John the Baptist officially identifying his cousin, saying, "This is the Lamb of God, who takes away the sin of the world!" (John 1:29)

And after his baptism, his heavenly Father sent down the Holy Spirit and said in a booming voice, "You are my Son, whom I love; with you I am well pleased" (Luke 3:22).

But what about you? Have you come to a place in your spiritual journey where you know for certain who Jesus is to you — not who he is to others, but to you? Not who sermons or spiritual books say that he is, but who he has come to be in your life?

We identify Jesus as our Lord by the personal things he has done in our lives, by the intimate words he has whispered, by the quiet miracles and the answered prayer. We can experience these things only when we have a genuine relationship with him. When we look at where we used to be and where we are today because of his mercy, that is when we are able to say, "My Lord and my God" (John 20:28).

To know Jesus as our Savior is to understand that he has saved us from our sin by his shed blood.

To know him as our Shepherd is to have experienced his guidance in our confusion.

To know him as our Rock and our Fortress is to know him as the one who saves us in battle and hides us from the storm.

To know him as our Friend is to have experienced his comfort in the midst of our loneliness.

Jesus is waiting to reveal himself to you as all of these things. He wants to be real and profoundly personal to you. Seek him in quiet times of prayer. Speak to him. Reveal your places of pain. Listen for his inner promptings. Read his Word. Let him work in your life.

And in time you will be able to say to him with joy and confidence as Nathanael did, "You are the Son of God; you are the King of Israel." But more than that, you will be able to say, "You are my Savior and my Friend."

Jesus, I have seen the face of your mercy. You are my Savior and my Friend. Lead me ever deeper into this life of faith. Amen.

Notes

Introduction
1. Richard J. Foster, *Prayer: Finding the Heart's True Home* (San Francisco: HarperSanFrancisco, 1992), p. 1.

Chapter 6
1. Frederick Buechner, *Telling the Truth: The Gospel as Tragedy, Comedy & Fairy Tale* (San Francisco: Harper and Row, 1977), p. 2.
2. Ibid., p. 7.

Chapter 10
1. Oswald Chambers, *Prayer: A Holy Occupation* (Grand Rapids, Mich.: Discovery House, 1992), p. 7.
2. Bill Hybels, *Too Busy Not to Pray: Slowing Down to Be with God* (Downers Grove, Ill.: InterVarsity Press, 1988), pp. 51–60.

Chapter 11
1. Wendell Berry, *Fidelity: Five Stories* (New York: Pantheon Books, 1992), p. 63.
2. Ibid., p. 71.

Chapter 24

1. Phil Ware, "Today's Verse from Heartlight," 3 October 2002. (http// www.heartlight.org)
2. Beth Moore, *Breaking Free: Making Liberty in Christ a Reality in Life* (Nashville, Tenn.: Lifeway Press, 1999), p. 199.

Chapter 27

1. Foster, *Prayer*, p. 191.

Chapter 41

1. Peggy Noonan, "You'd Cry Too, If It Happened to You," *Forbes*, September 1992.

Chapter 51

1. Foster, *Prayer*, p. 143.

Chapter 57

1. Andrew Murray, *The Prayer Life: The Inner Chamber and the Deepest Secret of Pentecost* (Pittsburgh, Pa: Whitaker House, 1981).

Chapter 62

1. Anne Ortlund, *Disciplines of the Beautiful Woman* (Waco, Tex.: Word Books, 1977), p. 51.

Chapter 75
1. Jeanie Miley, *Creative Silence* (Dallas: Word Publishing, 1989), p. 56.

Chapter 76
1. Brennan Manning, T.O.R., *The Gentle Revolutionaries: Breaking Through* (Denville, N.J.: Dimension Books, 1970), p. 25.

Chapter 97
1. Abbreviated paraphrase of blessing by Signa Bodishbaugh, *The Journey to Wholeness in Christ* (Grand Rapids, Mich.: Chosen Books, 1997), pp. 281–288. Revised and reprinted with permission.

Chapter 99
1. Henri J. M. Nouwen, *Life of the Beloved* (New York: Crossroad, 1992), p. 21.

Additional Copyright Information